Listen and[...]
for First
Certificate

John McDowell,
Lesley Denham and
Mike O'Neill

Edward Arnold

A division of Hodder & Stoughton

LONDON   MELBOURNE   AUCKLAND

Acknowledgements

The authors would like to thank Joy Morris for the ideas and suggestions she contributed to the structure and organisation of this book.

The authors and publishers would like to thank the following for permission to reproduce photographs, illustrations and text.

Barnaby's Picture Library, Pantek Arts, David Richardson.

Every effort has been made to contact copyright holders and apologies are made for any omissions.

© 1990 John McDowell, Lesley Denham and Mike O'Neill

First published in Great Britain 1990

British Library Cataloguing in Publication Data

McDowell, John, 1947–
   Listen and speak for first certificate.
   1. Spoken English language
   I. Title   II. Denham, Lesley   III. O'Neill, Mike
   428.3

   ISBN 0-340-52299-2

Typeset in 10/11 pt Rockwell by TecSet
Printed and bound in Great Britain by Thomson Litho Ltd, East Kilbride, Scotland for Edward Arnold, the educational, academic and medical publishing division of Hodder and Stoughton Limited, Mill Road, Dunton Green, Sevenoaks, Kent

Contents

| UNIT | TOPIC | LANGUAGE FOCUS AND DEVELOPMENT | |
		FUNCTIONAL	STRUCTURAL
1 The happiest days of your life	Education/ school days	Talk about the past	I remember my . . . We used to . . . When I was . . . In my experience . . . It is/was very different . . .
2 Keeping fit	Sports	Express uncertainty (when facts are not clear)	It looks as though . . . It looks as if . . . I think . . . Perhaps . . .
3 Appearances can be deceptive	Descriptions of people: – physical – character	Describe people	Adverbs of degree Wh-questions
4 Wanted!	Crime and delinquency	Hypothesise about what one would do Express opinions about what should be done	Conditional II, should/ought in active and passive
5 Something in the air	Pollution and ecology	Describing exact position in a photograph	It's in the foreground, background, etc.
6 What's on?	Entertainment	Express uncertainty (when facts are not clear)	It seems to be . . . I think it is . . . some sort of
7 The height of fashion	Fashion	Describe fashions Express preferences	Nouns/adjectives I prefer wearing . . . I'd rather wear . . . I'd buy . . .
8 All work and no play	Work/jobs	Express negative and positive aspects of a job	An advantage is . . . Comparatives
9 All creatures great and small	Animals	Describe and compare animals	Comparative Contrastive connectors
10 Dynasty	Family life	Talk about the past Talk about changes	Simple past used to . . . would . . . Present perfect has become/got
11 Getting away from it all	Travel	Describe and compare forms of transport	Comparative: a bit/ a lot/slightly/much
12 Time for a celebration	Religious festivals	Ask questions	Wh-questions Yes/No questions

COMMUNICATIVE TASK	EXAM STRATEGY	VOCABULARY TASK	LISTENING TASK	PAGE
Express preference Rank priorities Reach an agreement	Relate photograph to personal experience	Word association Linking words with images	True/false. Chart completion/gap-filling	1
Give and accept or reject advice	Describe (parts of) a photograph: people and actions	Form word sets Classify words	Chart completion (figures)	7
Talk about qualities of ideal partner	Infer from photo: feelings, thoughts. Understand how multiple-choice questions work	Identify antonyms	Multiple choice. Write multiple-choice questions	12
Discuss opinions on what should be done	Relate photograph to personal opinions	Match words with definitions	Matching exercise Gap filling	19
Reach agreement on course of action.	Identify parts of a photograph and position in the photograph	Infer meaning of words Use mind maps	Chart completion Answer questions	25
Reach agreement on plan	Using strategies to avoid difficult or unknown words	Gap-filling	True/false Dialogue completion	30
Argue about preferences and fashion	Explain reasons for liking photo Tackling multiple choice questions	Word game	Chart completion Multiple choice	35
Choose applicants for a job	Examine how a group interview works: who speaks to whom	Recycle known words and build up associations	Multiple choice Gap-filling	43
Discuss advantages and disadvantages	Anticipate examiner's questions Compare and contrast photographs	Match words and word classes	Gap-filling True/false	50
Discuss opinions of what should be done	Infer from photograph and relate it to own experience	Guess meaning of words in context	Chart completion Multiple choice	57
Choose and reach an agreement	Anticipate examiner's questions Compare and contrast photos	Anagrams True/false	Matching exercise	64
Choose and reach an agreement	Anticipate examiner's questions Focus on how to answer questions	Strategies to learn new words	Find differences Gap filling	71

Introduction

Listen and Speak for First Certificate is a course consisting of a student's book and a cassette. It prepares learners for papers 4 and 5 of the University of Cambridge First Certificate examination by providing thorough and motivating training in the skills and language needed for the examination. It also provides interesting material for language improvement in general.

What does the book help me with?

The material is designed to help you revise the language you already know and learn more. It also helps you to improve your general learning skills and to develop specific strategies to cope with the *First Certificate* examination.

What specific aspects of language and learning skills will I learn?

The book contains material and tasks to help you with:

Vocabulary: There is a wide variety of exercises to help you **both** revise and remember the words you already know **and** to learn new words

Grammar: Each unit focuses on specific aspects of grammar. You have the chance to study different language structures and to use them in communicative situations.

Listening: There is a varied selection of recorded material to accompany each unit. As well as exercises that focus on aspects of language, there are also tasks to help you improve your listening skills. These tasks are based on the kind you will meet in the First Certificate examination.

Speaking: There are tasks to help you to improve your ability to keep up a conversation of the kind involved in the examination.

Learning skills: You will find exercises to encourage you to think about strategies you can use to learn more. For example, you will learn how to acquire more vocabulary, or how to judge and assess your performance.

Examination skills: In each unit throughout the book there are activities to help you to be more successful in the examination. For example, you will find tasks to develop your ability to:
- think of things to say
- carry on a natural conversation
- anticipate what the examiner expects
- avoid words and expressions you do not know
- look for the right answer in listening tasks

How do I use the book?

The book consists of twelve units with accompanying recorded material on cassette. Each unit is organised around a theme or topic, but there is no grading or order of difficulty. You can therefore use the units in any order, depending on the topics that most interest you. At the beginning of the book you will find an index with information about the topic and language contained in each unit.

The material is designed to be used by learners working either in class with a teacher or on their own in a group (for example, in a self-access centre). The approach emphasises the co-operative aspect of learning and, whether you are working with or without a teacher, you should try to take an **active** approach to each task and to help each other. An important aspect of this is self-evaluation and evaluation of others, which will help you improve your ability to learn more and to perform in the examination. There is a self-evaluation chart on page xiv. A key with answers to the tasks is available on request from the publishers.

How do I use the material in each unit?

Each unit consists of six sections, each focussing on different aspects of language and learning. You should work through each section in order.

SECTION 1 Vocabulary Development

The exercises in this section help you to revise and learn the words you need to talk about the topic of the unit. There are also exercises to give you strategies for learning and recording new words.

SECTION 2 Language Focus

This section deals with specific aspects of grammar or language structure. The aim is to present you with samples of language and encourage you to discover how the language works and when you can use it.

SECTION 3 Language Application

This section is closely linked to the previous one. Here, you have the chance to use the language from section 2 in communicative situations of the kind you will find in the examinations.

SECTION 4 Text Identification

In this section you will get practice at recognising written texts and guessing their context, a task that you are required to do in the examination. The texts are linked to the topic and material of the unit. You will find a chart on page 81 to be used with this section.

SECTION 5 Listening

Each unit contains two sets of listening tasks of the kind you will find in the First Certificate examination. The topic of each task is based on the topic of the unit. You will practise and improve your listening skills and also acquire strategies to cope with the type of task normally found in the examination.

SECTION 6 Speaking

This section gives you practice in carrying on the type of conversation required in the interview. The book contains a wide variety of task types, including discussion, role play, problem solving, etc.

How do I develop specific strategies for the examination?

The material in the book provides a variety of exercises and tasks to help you focus on strategies to help you cope in the examination. These appear regularly throughout the book.

An important element to help you prepare for the examination is the self-evaluation chart on page xiv. This is provided for you to use with the tasks in section 3 and, especially, section 6. The instructions in these sections ask you to refer to the chart. Normally, the instructions require one student to take the part of the examiner, organising the activity **and** using the chart to assess the other students. By doing this you will understand better what the examiners are looking for and be able to perform better in their presence.

What exactly will the examination be like?

In this book you will find a section giving you information about the procedures of the examination (page ix) and another section giving you specific hints on how to cope (page x).

What happens in the oral examination?

Individual oral

This will last between ten and twelve minutes. When you enter the room the examiner will welcome you and ask a few introductory questions to help you relax.

The examiner will then give you one or more photographs. The subject of the photograph will depend on what theme the examiner has chosen to talk to you about. Cambridge provides the examiners with different materials based on themes. The examiner will then ask you questions about the photograph. The possible types of question and the language you may need for this part of the examination are dealt with in Section 2 of each unit of this book.

Photograph

The examiner may then give you a short passage to read silently to yourself and then ask you some questions about it. Examples of the types of passage and question you may be asked are dealt with in Section 4 of each unit of this book.

The last section of the oral examination may be a discussion, role play or a problem-solving exercise. Examples of the types of activity you may be given are dealt with in Section 6 of each unit of this book.

The marks for the oral examination are divided into six categories. For more details see the chart on page xiv. The oral examination has a total of 40 marks out of an overall total of 180 for the whole First Certificate examination. You generally need 100 marks to pass the examination.

Group oral

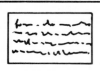

Passage

This will last about twenty minutes. You will do the examination with one or two other candidates. When you enter the room the examiner will welcome you and ask a few introductory questions to help you relax. He or she may ask these individually or ask the members of the group to introduce themselves to each other.

The examiner will then give you a photograph to look at. You may all have the same photograph or different ones. These will be based on a theme. Cambridge provides the examiners with different materials based on themes. He or she will ask you questions about the photographs or possibly ask you to compare them if they are different. The types of question and the language you may need for this part of the examination are dealt with in Section 2 of each unit of the book.

The examiner may then give you a short passage to read silently to yourself and ask you some questions about it. You may have the same passage or different ones. Examples of the types of passage and question you may be asked are dealt with in Section 4 of each unit of this book.

The last section of the examination may be a discussion, a role play or a problem-solving exercise. This activity involves the candidates only and the examiner will not usually take part. Examples of the types of activity you may be given are dealt with in Section 6 of each unit of this book.

The marks for the oral examination are divided into six categories. For more details see the chart on page xiv. The oral examination has a total of

40 marks out of an overall total of 180 for the whole First Certificate examination. You generally need 100 marks to pass the examination.

Orals based on a set book

If you have studied one of the set books during the year you can choose to talk about it during the interview. The format of the examination remains the same but all the material is based on the book.
- The photographs will be related to the book: for example, a picture of the book cover.
- The short passages will be taken from the text of the book.
- In the final part of the interview you will be asked general questions about the book. These questions are usually related to the characters in the story or general themes in the book.

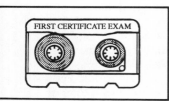

This is a cassette

An examination paper – the front.

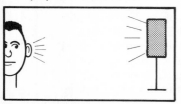

A speaker and a student listening.

What happens in the listening examination?

You will usually take the listening examination with a larger group of candidates in one room. The listening texts are recorded on a cassette. The invigilators will first give you instructions and test the sound quality of the cassette before you start the examination. You will then be able to ask questions if you are not sure about the instructions. The invigilator then gives you the examination paper.

The examination paper will have three or four different parts with different types of listening exercise. Examples of the types of exercise you may have are given in Section 5 of each unit of this book.

The invigilator will then start the cassette. Once the cassette starts the invigilator cannot stop it. You will hear the text for each part of the examination twice. After the first hearing you will be given a short time to look at your answers before you hear the same text again. At the end of the examination you will have a short time to check your answers before the invigilator collects the answer papers.

The listening examination has a total of 20 marks out of an overall total of 180 for the whole First Certificate examination. You generally need 100 marks to pass the examination.

The above descriptions of the oral and listening examinations follow an outline which Cambridge gives examiners. Conditions will not be exactly the same in all the examination centres so if you have any questions ask your teacher or the examination centre where you will take the First Certificate examination.

Tips for the oral examination

Here are some problems that students have had with the oral examination. Read them and think about what you would do if it happened to you. Discuss them with another student.

'I was so nervous at the beginning that I could hardly say my name!'
'I looked at the photograph and realised I didn't know the word for something.'
'The picture was so boring that I couldn't think of anything to say.'
'I didn't understand the question the examiner asked me.'
'When I was speaking I suddenly realised I couldn't think of a word I needed.'
'The other students in the group were speaking all the time and didn't give me a chance to say anything.'

Tips

- The majority of students are very nervous when they enter the examination room but they usually relax as time passes. The examiner will not be marking your English from the minute you enter the room but will help you relax first, so do not worry if you are very nervous at the beginning. Greet the examiner when you walk in and use his/her introductory questions to help you relax.
- If you do not know a word for something, do not panic! The examiner realises that you are probably nervous. If you think it is *very* important then you can ask the examiner. You do not lose marks because you do not know the exact word. Another solution is to avoid using the word by giving a definition or explanation of it. This is practised in Unit 6 of this book.
- The examiner uses the photograph to start the conversation. If you cannot think of anything to say, the examiner will help you by asking further questions. Talk about the subject in general, not only about the contents of the photograph, or try to relate it to your personal experience. Try not to give short answers like 'yes' and 'no' because the examiner has to hear you speak before he or she can give you a mark.
- If you don't understand the examiner then ask her/him to repeat. Prepare the language for this before you do the examination.
- When you are nervous you often cannot remember quite common words and the examiner realises this. What you often need is just a few seconds to think. In your own language you have words, noises or expressions that give you time to think and organise your ideas. In English there are similar words and noises. Do you know what they are? Look at the list at the end of this section.
- If there is a dominant candidate in your group then the examiner will make sure that the other candidate/s has/have a chance to speak. However, you can learn some interruption techniques so you can join in the conversation in a natural way. Can you think of any ways to interrupt a person politely? Look at the list below.

Pause words to give you time to think

Well...	The thing is... er...
Let me see...	Er, well, yes...
Umm, what's it called... oh yes...	So... umm...
Oh well, really...	

Interruption techniques
Sorry to interrupt but . . .
Yes, but . . .
I'd just like to say that . . .
Do you really think so? I think that . . .

General tips for the individual oral

- You are with the examiner for a very short time so try within that time to show that you know a range of vocabulary and expressions. If you know that you have favourite expressions or words that you use a lot try to learn different ones. Sections 1 and 2 in the units of this book will introduce you to new vocabulary and expressions, so try to use them.
- Remember that there is no 'correct answer' when you are discussing opinions. What is important is to have ideas to express.
- If you are talking about the set book during the interview, do not 'prepare' what you are going to say and then repeat it in the examination. Prepare some relevant vocabulary but do not become too inflexible.

General tips for the group interview

- You may not know the other candidate/s in your group so use the time for introductions to relax and practise some easy questions.
- In the group examination, the conversation takes place mainly between the candidates, not between each individual candidate and the examiner. This is particularly true of the last part of the interview. When the other candidate/s is/are talking, listen to them. Do not sit and wait for your turn to speak. Remember that speaking involves listening to the other person and reacting/responding. As you would in a conversation in your own language, show that you are listening by gestures or words of agreement or surprise.

Tips for the listening examination

During the listening examination you have no gestures or facial expressions to help you understand what the people are saying. Because of this it is very important that you prepare for what you are going to hear. You can do this in the following ways:

- When the invigilator tells you that you can look at the paper, look quickly at each section so that you are familiar with the type of exercise it is – a multiple choice, an information gap, etc.
- Before you hear each section of the examination there is a short pause on the cassette. Use this time to look at the questions you have to answer. Try to see what the subject of the passage is so that you are prepared for vocabulary related to that area. There is an exercise to help you with this in Unit 7 of this book.
- In an information gap exercise, look for what type of information you need to complete the spaces. Is it numbers, names or dates? Be prepared when you see exercises involving numbers or letters. The examiner will usually choose ones that are easily confused. Make sure

you can distinguish between, for example, 13/30, 14/40, 15/50, etc. and the vowels a/e/i/o/u. Practise numbers and alphabet when you have some free time in class or at home.

- In a multiple-choice question there is only one right answer. The other possibilities are there to distract you. Be careful with these distractors. There is an exercise in Unit 3 of this book to help you understand the idea behind this type of question.

When you do the listening exercises in Section 5 of each unit, practise preparing yourself for the subject of the passage and the type of information you have to listen for.

Self-Assessment

In the examination, the examiner assesses different aspects of your English. These are:

- **Fluency**: this refers to your ability to speak in a connected way without too much hesitation or stopping to look for words and expressions. It does not mean that you have to talk very fast – you should try to speak at a natural speed with a steady, comfortable rhythm.
- **Grammatical accuracy**: this refers to how many grammatical mistakes you make (verbs, prepositions, grammar structures, tenses, etc.).
- **Pronunciation: sentences**: this refers to how well you use intonation, how well you link phrases and the general rhythm of your sentences.
- **Pronunciation: individual sounds**: this refers to how well you pronounce all the individual sounds of English.
- **Interactive communication**: this refers to your ability to keep up a conversation – how well you initiate conversation, understand other people, respond, keep the conversation going.
- **Vocabulary resource**: this refers to how wide your vocabulary is and to your ability to find the words to talk about concrete and abstract subjects.

The examiner will give you a mark from 1 to 5 for each of these points.

When you are doing the activities in this book, use the chart below to assess your English. Put a circle round a mark for each aspect. If you find it difficult to think of all the points at the same time, choose just two or three to focus on.

Self-assessment chart					
Fluency	1	2	3	4	5
Grammatical accuracy	1	2	3	4	5
Pronunciation: sentences	1	2	3	4	5
Pronunciation: individual sounds	1	2	3	4	5
Interactive communication	1	2	3	4	5
Vocabulary resource	1	2	3	4	5

UNIT 1 | The happiest days of your life?

Section 1 Vocabulary development

Exercise 1 Without thinking for more than two seconds, what is the first word that comes into your head when you read the word 'blue'? Discuss and explain your answers with a partner.

Exercise 2 Now look at the blackboard below on the left and choose one of the words written on it. Without thinking for a long time, write a word on the blackboard on the right which you associate with this word. Do this exercise individually, as the word that comes into your mind may not be the same as another student's.

When you have seven words on each blackboard, discuss your choice of words with another student or students.

Exercise 3 Look at the words and expressions below and make sure you understand them. (They are all related to education.)

revision	term	timetable	mark	strict
report	corporal	punishment	play	truant

Work in pairs and match each of the words above with a word from the blackboards. Give reasons for your choice.

Exercise 4   Remembering new vocabulary can be a big problem! In the previous discussion about education did you come across any new words? What were they? One way of helping you remember new words is to create a strong image of them in your mind. Choose some of the new words you have come across in this unit and draw a picture below, which, to you, represents that word. Write the new word, without a translation, next to the image.

Have a look at some of the other students' drawings. Are they the same as yours?

Section 2   Language focus

Exercise 1   Look at the photograph below and listen to the person on the cassette comparing it with his experience at school. As you listen, complete the table on the next page with the differences between his experience and the situation shown in the photograph.

Photograph	Candidate's experience
Students in the geography class look very serious.	Geography classes were not so serious

Exercise 2   Now listen to the cassette again and write down all the expressions the candidate uses to relate the picture to his own experience. The first one is written here:

> I remember my . . .

Section 3   Language application

Look at the photograph on the previous page and try to compare it with your experience at school. Work in pairs, one of you taking the part of the examiner and the other the part of the candidate. If you can, record the interview and then listen to it and assess yourself using the self-assessment chart on page xiv.

Section 4   Text identification

Where would you expect to find these texts? Look at the check-list on page 81 and tick (√) the appropriate features. Then answer the questions following the check-list. Finally, look at the photographs in this unit. Do you think the texts could refer to them or any of the people shown? How?

Text 1   Well, Mr Hardwood, since I last saw you about your daughter's work I'm pleased to say that there has been a great improvement in both her attitude and behaviour. She is working much harder now and is generally being more co-operative. She still needs to concentrate on improving her science subjects but apart from that I'm happy with her progress.

Text 2   In a recent study made by sociologists, it has been shown that corporal punishment is still widely present in schools today. Many institutions claim that this is the only way to control disobedient school children from inner-city areas where the problem seems to be the greatest. Headmasters from these areas are deeply concerned about the deterioration in standards of behaviour.

The examiner may ask you more questions about the texts. Look at the questions below and discuss them in pairs or small groups.

Text 1:
Did/do your parents go to your school to talk about your work? How did/do you feel?
What subjects did/do you like most and least at school? Why?

Text 2:
Do you think corporal punishment is an effective way of trying to solve discipline problems? What alternatives are there?
Do you think there are more discipline problems in schools today than before?

Section 5   Listening

Listening task 1   On the cassette you will hear the welcoming speech of the principal of a language school in England to students who have just arrived for a summer course. Put a tick (√) in the appropriate columns to say whether the following statements are true or false.

	True	False
1 A summer course lasts one month.	✓	
2 The students already know who their class teachers are.		✓
3 The students have already been on a sightseeing tour of the area.		✓
4 All students have to do a project on the history of the school.		✓
5 There is a new computer room.	✓	
6 Classes begin at 9.00 a.m.		✓
7 The social activities programme is not compulsory.	✓	
8 The school is in a big city.		✓
9 The disco begins at 9.30 p.m.		✓

Listening task 2   On the cassette you will hear a parent discussing his son's school report with his tutor. Listen and complete the blanks in the report below.

End of Year Report

Name: Stephen Jameson   **Class**:   (1) _4A_   **Age**:   14

Subject	Exam result	Comment
Mathematics	(2) _60%_	A satisfactory year's work. The only problem area is his algebra.
(3) _History_	48%	Stephen needs to concentrate more in class. He seems to have a very poor (4) _memory_
Music	40%	Stephen is far too (5) _talkative_ in class and he is not taking his (6) _guitar_ lessons seriously.
Geography	64%	He has improved a lot this year and his project on (7) _China_ was excellent.
(8) _Art_	58%	I am happy to see a great improvement in Stephen's work this year. He seemed to become very interested after our visit to the local (9) _art gallery_
French	(10) _80%_	Well done! An excellent year's work. The trip to France at (11) _Easter_ helped his oral work a lot.

Section 6   Problem solving

Look at the list below of possible facilities for a language school in England. Work in small groups and discuss the facilities, putting them in order of importance. Before you start the discussion spend a few minutes preparing your own ideas.

Television and video room
Cafeteria
Computer room
Minibus (for trips)
Games room (for example, table tennis)
Study centre
Language laboratory
Large room (for drama classes, discos, etc.)
Membership of the local sports centre

Look at the language below and try to use some of it during the discussion.

> I think a(an) *x* is more important than a(an) *y*.
> I'd prefer to have . . .
> I think it would be a good idea to have a . . .
> As far as I'm concerned a . . .
> How do you feel about a . . .?
> I think so, too.
> Yes, but . . .

Either:
Record the discussion on a cassette. When you have finished, listen to the recording and use the form on page xiv to assess your performance.
Or:
Choose one person in the group to act as examiner. The examiner's role is to stimulate the discussion if necessary, to make sure that everyone in the group has a chance to speak, etc. **and** to use the form on page xiv to assess the students' performance. At the end of the discussion the examiner should discuss the assessment with the group.

Keeping fit

Section 1 Vocabulary development

Work in pairs. First group these words according to the sport you associate them with, and then add as many more words as you can. Then work with another pair and compare and extend your lists.

deuce   bat   half-time   court   net   stadium   glove
rink   racket   ring   kick   sprint   jump

For example:

Boxing	Cricket	Tennis	Athletics	Ice hockey	Football
glove ring					

Section 2 Language focus

Exercise 1

Look at the photograph and notice that it has been divided into different areas. Listen to the person on the cassette describing the photograph and make a note of the areas she describes and in what order. Why did she describe them in this order?

Exercise 2   The speaker uses different structures and expressions to express uncertainty, for example: *it looks as though* . . .

Can you think of any others? Work with a partner and make a note of the ones you can think of. Then, listen to the cassette and make a note of all the other expressions and structures the speaker uses to express uncertainty.

Exercise 3   Work with a partner. Without looking at the list of expressions you made in Exercise 2, say as many sentences as you can about the photograph using expressions of uncertainty.

Section 3   Language Application

Exercise 1   Now look at these two photographs. Work with a partner and make a list of all the words you would need to describe them. Then write down a few sentences expressing uncertainty: use some of the structures you learned in Section 2.

Exercise 2 Divide the photographs into areas like those in the photograph in Section 2. Work with a partner and discuss how to do it.

Exercise 3 Describe one of the photographs to your partner using the different areas you have marked. Your partner will have to decide which photograph you are describing. Then change roles.

Section 4 Text identification

Where would you expect to find these texts? Look at the check-list on page 81 and tick (√) the appropriate features. Then answer the questions following the check-list. Finally, look at the photographs in this unit. Do you think the texts could refer to them or to any of the people shown? How?

Text 1 Well, there's nothing actually wrong with you, Mr Williams. The back pain you have been having is probably due to lack of exercise. I would advise you to spend a few minutes each morning doing these simple exercises on this chart. I think you'll soon find the aches disappear. Meanwhile, I'll prescribe some pills for you to take.

Text 2 Wimbledon   0
Luton Town   1
Three things spoiled this match. One was the football itself, which was dreadful; the second was the decision by the Luton goalkeeper not to do with the replacement ball what he had done with the original, which was to boot it out of the ground; and third was the smoke that drifted across the ground towards the end and did not totally obliterate it.

The examiner may ask you more questions about the texts. Look at the questions below and discuss them in pairs or small groups.

Text 1:
What kind of pills do you think they are? What are they for?
Have you ever suffered from back pain? What was it like?
Do you do any kind of regular exercise? What?

Text 2:
Most football commentators are men. Why do you think this is?
Why did the commentator want the smoke to obliterate the ground?
How do you know he is being sarcastic?

🖭 Section 5 Listening

Listening task 1 Listen to the couple, John and Pam, on the cassette talking about a skiing trip they are going on with their small son, Tommy. As you listen, look at the items below and write BR beside the ones they are going to borrow, BY beside the ones they are going to buy and HR beside the ones they are going to hire. They already have some of the things: in this case leave the space blank.

	John	Pam	Tommy
1			
2			
3			
4			

Listening task 2   Listen to the results of the radio questionnaire on sport and physical exercise and complete the chart below.

Activities	% Men	% Women
Physical exercise	40	(1) _____
Watch sport on TV	41	(2) _____
Jogging	20	(3) _____
Football	(4) _____	None
(5) _____	19	None
Walking	(6) _____	90
Athletics	(7) _____	None
Dancing	3	(8) _____
(9) _____	2	5
(10) _____	11	13

Section 6   Role play

Work in pairs, student A and student B, and choose a role each (doctor and patient). Read your role card and then role-play the conversation between the doctor and the patient.

Doctor	Patient
Your patient has backache. You think there is nothing serious so you recommend regular exercise. You know your patient doesn't like exercise but you try to convince him/her to do a little. Any of the following are useful: jogging, simple physical exercises at home, swimming, yoga, walking.	You have had backache for a long time. You lead a very sedentary life and never do any exercise. In fact you do not like exercise. Your doctor has just examined you and thinks you need to do regular exercise. He suggests some possibilities but you find disadvantages to all of them.

Before you start, make notes on the following factors:

Price	Time
Effect	Equipment
Availability	Team or individual

Either:
Record the discussion on a cassette. When you have finished, listen to the recording and use the form on page xiv to assess your performance.
Or:
Assign one person to each pair to act as examiner. The examiner's role is to stimulate the discussion if necessary, to make sure that each person has a chance to speak, etc. **and** to use the form on page xiv to assess the students' performance. At the end of the discussion the examiner should discuss the assessment with the pair.

 **UNIT 3** Appearances can be deceptive

Section 1 Vocabulary development

Exercise 1 Work in pairs. One of you should look at box A and cover up box B and the other should look at box B and cover up box A. The student looking at box A then says one of the words in the box and the other student then has to say a word from box B meaning the opposite. You continue in this way until you have made pairs with all the words. Finally, look at both boxes.

Box A

elegant	insensitive	formal
ugly	pessimistic	extrovert
open-minded	unreliable	insecure
serious	slim	patient

Box B

overweight	informal	confident
understanding	reliable	narrow-minded
light-hearted	untidy	shy
optimistic	good-looking	short-tempered

Exercise 2 Which of the words above would you use to describe yourself? Discuss your choice with a partner.

Section 2 Language focus

Exercise 1 Look at the photographs of people below and listen to the candidate describing them on the cassette. Make a note of the order in which she describes them and write down all the words she uses from boxes A and B above.

Exercise 2   When we describe people, we often use adverbs of degree with the adjective, for example:

He's *rather* serious.

She looks *incredibly* intelligent.

Listen to the interview again and make a note of all the adverbs of degree you can hear.

Exercise 3   Look at the photograph below of two more people. The examiner will sometimes ask you to imagine information about the people rather than talk about the actual contents of the photograph, for example:

What do you think is the relationship between the people in the photograph?

Why do you think they look so nervous/happy/sad?

Work in groups of four; two of you are pair A and the other two, pair B. Both pairs write three questions about the photograph below, asking what the people are thinking or feeling. Begin your questions with 'How', 'What', and 'Why'.

Then work in pairs, one student A with one student B, and ask each other the questions.

Section 3   Language application

Work in pairs. One of you takes the role of the examiner and the other that of the candidate. Look at the first photograph opposite and follow the instructions on your role card. Then change roles and talk about the second photograph. If you can, record the interview and then listen to it and assess yourself using the self-assessment chart on page xiv.

<table>
<tr><td>

Candidate

Think about the words you could use from boxes A and B above to describe the person. Which adverbs of degree would combine with these words? Then answer the examiner's questions.

</td><td>

Examiner

Think about questions to ask the candidate about the person's appearance and what she is thinking or feeling. Then ask the questions.

</td></tr>
</table>

Section 4   Text identification

Where would you expect to find these texts? Look at the check-list on page 81 and tick (√) the appropriate features. Then answer the questions following the check-list. Finally, look at the photographs in this unit. Do you think the texts could refer to them or any of the people shown? How?

Text 1   ... and all of you born under this sign are going to have an extremely good month. The moon is in line with the planets which means you will be lucky in love and money. There's only one thing to watch out for: a bit of trouble with other members of the family who could be slightly jealous of your financial success. Lucky days are the 12th and 22nd. Be careful on the 16th of a voice from the past.

Text 2   I remember the evening that Sarah introduced me to Paul. It was at a party.
    'Paul, this is Kathy. Kathy, this is Paul.'
    'Pleased to meet you,' he said. I remember his voice; it was friendly. He was tall and his eyes were dark, dark brown. In fact they were almost black. I liked him immediately.

The examiner may ask you more questions about the texts. Look at the questions below and discuss them in pairs or small groups.

Text 1:
Do you read your horoscope? Do you believe in it?
Do you think that a person's character is influenced by the sign they are born under?

Text 2:
Look at the photographs of people in this unit. Which one do you think could be Paul?
What do you think happens to Kathy and Paul in the story?
Do you think first impressions of people are important?

Section 5   Listening

Listening task 1   Listen to two employers on the cassette talking about a man they have just interviewed for a job with their company. Read the following questions and choose the correct answer in each case.

1   They are worried that Mr Johnson
    (a) has not had enough relevant experience.
    (b) has not got enough qualifications.
    (c) is over qualified.
    (d) has changed job too often in the past.

2   The most important thing about the person they employ is that
    (a) he has dealt with large groups of people before.
    (b) he has attended a managerial course.
    (c) he can organise a managerial course.
    (d) he is willing to be flexible.

3   The interviewee's present employer said
    (a) he always arrived at work on time.
    (b) he was flexible about when he left work.
    (c) he was a clock-watcher.
    (d) he left on time because he had a long journey home.

4   The interviewee thought that
    (a) being reliable was more important than being well dressed.
    (b) staff should talk to managers about work problems only.
    (c) politeness was quite important.
    (d) a manager should have the confidence of his staff.

5   The two employers decide
    (a) to give him a six-month trial period.
    (b) to arrange a second interview.
    (c) to re-advertise the job.
    (d) to look at the other applications for another suitable candidate.

Listening task 2   In the First Certificate listening examination there is usually a multiple-choice test like the one you practised above. In each case, there is only one correct answer and the other three possibilities are there to distract you. These distractors usually use words from the text but the information is not totally correct.

For the exercise below, imagine you are the First Certificate examiner and you are preparing a multiple-choice test for Cambridge. Work in groups of four; two of you are pair A and the other two pair B. Pair A should look at page 89 and read the text for the listening comprehension. Pair B should look at the same page and read the text that has been printed upside down. (Do not read each other's text!)

Prepare four possible answers for the questions below. Pair A should prepare questions 1 and 2, and pair B numbers 3 and 4. When you have finished, copy the other pair's questions. Then listen to the cassette and choose the correct answers. Finally, check your answers with the other pair.

1   This week Aquarians will be
    (a)
    (b)
    (c)
    (d)

2   During the coming week Pisceans should
    (a)
    (b)
    (c)
    (d)

3   In the recent past, Aries have been
    (a)
    (b)
    (c)
    (d)

4   The people Taureans may meet next week
   (a)
   (b)
   (c)
   (d)

When you have finished the listening tasks, read the tapescripts and make a note of any new words to describe people's appearance or personality.

Section 6   Role play

First work individually. Imagine that you are going to a marriage bureau to find your ideal partner. Think about what kind of person this would be. Make a few notes on the person's appearance and personality. Try to use some of the new vocabulary that you have learnt in this unit.

Then work in pairs. One of you is the person who works at the bureau and the other the person who is looking for their ideal partner. Role play the situation. Then change roles and repeat the exercise. In the box below you will find some useful language to use during the role play.

> I'd like him/her to be . . .
> I think it's important that he/she is . . .
> He/she should be . . .
> I don't want someone who is . . .
> Do you really think so?
> I couldn't agree more!

Either:
Record the discussion on a cassette. When you have finished, listen to the recording and use the form on page xiv to assess your performance.
   Or:
Work in groups of three with one person in each group taking the role of examiner. The examiner's role is to stimulate the conversation if necessary, **and** to use the form on page xiv to assess the students' performance. At the end of the role play the examiner should discuss the assessment with the other two students.

UNIT 4 | Wanted!

Section 1 Vocabulary development

Look at this list of crimes. Read the examples and definitions below and match the crime with the definition:

(a) robbery   (e) murder   (h) mugging
(b) burglary   (f) embezzlement   (i) assassination
(c) kidnapping   (g) arson   (j) shoplifting
(d) hijacking

1 A building is deliberately burnt down.
2 Things are stolen from a house.
3 An employee steals money regularly from the company he works for.
4 A person is attacked in the street and robbed of his money.
5 Terrorists take control of a plane and threaten to kill the passengers.
6 A famous politician is shot and killed.
7 Two men hold up a bank and steal £10,000.
8 A person steals a shirt from a department store.
9 The man attacked in the street dies later in hospital.
10 A rich woman is taken by force from her home. The criminals demand money from her family.

🔲 Section 2 Language focus

Exercise 1 Look at the picture below. On the cassette, the examiner asks the candidate:

What would you do if this happened to you?

What do you think the candidate will say?
What other information will she give?
How do you think the conversation will continue?

Exercise 2 Listen to the first part of the interview and check your predictions. Then listen again and answer these questions:

What would she do?
Why?
How would she feel?
Has it ever happened to her in real life?
Does this happen often in her town/country?

Exercise 3 Work in pairs and practise the same kind of conversation with these pictures. One student takes the part of the examiner and the other the part of the candidate. Change roles for each picture. The examiner can ask the questions in Exercise 2.

Exercise 4 Now you are going to hear the next part of the interview. Look back at the picture in Exercise 1. The examiner asks:

What do you think should happen to the man in the picture?

Listen and circle which of these sentences the candidate says.

he should be arrested   he should be put in prison
they should put him in prison   he should be fined
they should help him find a job   they should arrest him
they ought to fine him   he ought to be helped

Exercise 5 Now work in pairs. Look at the pictures in Exercise 3 and say what you think should happen to the criminal(s).

Section 3   Language application

Look at this picture. Work in pairs or small groups. One of you takes the part of the examiner and the others are candidates. Develop a conversation about what you would do if you found yourself in the situation of the woman in the picture and say what you think should happen to the kidnappers. Use Section 2 as a model.

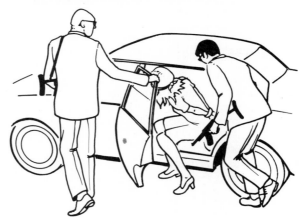

Section 4   Text identification

Where would you expect to find these texts? Look at the check-list on page 81 and tick (√) the appropriate features. Then answer the questions following the check-list. Finally, look at the pictures in this unit. Do you think the texts could refer to them or any of the people shown? How?

Text 1 J. W. RANDALL & SON OFFER A REWARD OF £1000 FOR ANY INFORMATION LEADING TO THE ARREST AND CONVICTION OF THE PERPETRATORS OF A RAID CARRIED OUT ON THEIR SHOP IN HIGH STREET, WELBY, ON MONDAY 6th JUNE at 11.00 a.m. ALL CALLS WILL BE TREATED IN STRICTEST CONFIDENCE.

Text 2

Tuesday 10th

plane 4·05   airport 2·45

to do:
- cancel milk and papers
- tell neighbours about going away
- turn off gas and electricity
- leave hall light on ????
- leave address with Jean
- connect answerphone ????

The examiner may ask you more questions about the texts. Look at the questions below and discuss them in pairs or small groups.

Text 1:
Do you think it is a good idea for the police to offer public money as a reward for information? Why (not)? What would you do if you had information about the raid?

Text 2:
What precautions can you take to avoid being robbed in the street/on public transport/at a sports event? What about your car: how can you try to protect it from thieves?

🖭 Section 5   Listening

Listening task 1   Look at the five photographs opposite. Then listen to the cassette and decide which two men are being described.

Listening task 2   Listen to the interview on the cassette between a Police Inspector and a witness to a robbery and then fill in the information missing below:

1   The first police interview with Mr Wilson took place on:

    _____, _____ _____
    (day)   (date) (month)

2   The registration number given by Wilson to the police was:

    — — — — — — —

3   Mr Wilson had just bought some _____ from the _____ when he saw the robbery.

4   On that day:

    the robbery took place at _____ p.m.

    the chemist's closed at _____ p.m.

5   There were _____ members of the gang responsible for the robbery.

    So far, the police have arrested _____ of them.

Section 6   Discussion

Work in pairs or small groups and discuss the topic below:

> What is the best thing to do with criminals:
> punish them or help them to reform? How?

Before you start, spend a few minutes thinking about the following points:
different types of criminal
different reasons for their crimes
violent vs. non-violent criminals/crimes
different forms of punishment: fine, work in the community, prison, penalty, etc.
ways to help criminals reform

Either:
Record the discussion on a cassette. When you have finished, listen to the recording and use the form on page xiv to assess your performance.
Or:
Choose one person in the group to act as examiner. The examiner's role is to stimulate the discussion if necessary, to make sure that everyone in the group has a chance to speak, etc. **and** to use the form on page xiv to assess the students' performance. At the end of the discussion the examiner should discuss the assessment with the group.

Something in the air

Section 1   Vocabulary development

Exercise 1   Look at the words and expressions below and see how many you understand. Do not ask for any help or use a dictionary yet! Do you know how to pronounce them?

> carbon monoxide   aerosols   lead-free petrol   exhaust fumes
> chemical waste   radioactive waste   contaminate   dump
> litter   ozone layer   pollution   power stations

Exercise 2   Read this short passage about the environment and underline the words above.

> The increase in the number of private cars on the road today is one of the factors contributing to the pollution problem in our inner cities. If private car owners, transport firms and public transport could be persuaded to change to lead-free petrol then the amount of carbon monoxide from exhaust fumes would be reduced. Factories also contaminate our air, sea and rivers with chemical waste despite government warnings. Nuclear power stations continue to dump their radioactive waste into the sea threatening many species of fish. People are also responsible for contributing to the polluting of the atmosphere; smoking is just one example of this. Another is the use of aerosols which damage the ozone layer around the earth. And regarding visual pollution, people have still got a lot to learn as, wherever you go for that idyllic picnic, there is nearly always some litter left behind by a previous group.

Exercise 3   Study the words in context and see if you now understand them. Check them with another student. (Check the pronunciation as well as the meaning.)

Exercise 4   Now look at the diagram on page 26. The main topic is written in the centre: pollution. Around it there are the four causes of pollution mentioned in the passage above. First work individually and, following the example, connect words from the passage to the four causes to show how they pollute the environment. Then compare your diagram with a partner's and discuss any words you still do not understand.

The diagram is a small 'mind map' of words related to pollution. This is a way of keeping a note of vocabulary in your notebook. As you go through this unit, add any new words you find.

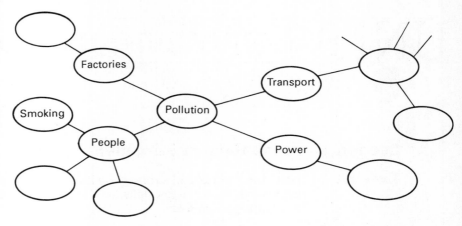

These maps can be used to keep a record of vocabulary or for organising your ideas for a composition for Paper Two of the First Certificate examination. For example, the 'map' above could be a plan for a composition on the causes of pollution. Remember always to put the central idea in the middle and build out from that, using different colours for each idea if possible. The 'maps' can look very attractive when you finish!

Section 2   Language focus

The picture below has some crosses (x) marked on it. Listen to the person on the cassette describing it and make a note of the words and expressions she uses to describe the position of each of the marked places. Write the words on the empty picture frame opposite. Then check your answers with the tapescript on page 91.

in the foreground

Now add any positions which were not mentioned on the cassette.

Section 3 Language application

Work in pairs, student A and student B. Student A should look at the picture on page 80 and dictate the position of the objects to student B, who should try to draw the picture in the empty frame above. Use the language from Section 2 to explain the position of the objects.

When you have finished, student B should look at the picture on page 82 and dictate it to student A in the same way as above.

Finally check the position of the objects by looking at the original pictures.

Section 4 Text identification

Where would you expect to find these texts? Look at the check-list on page 81 and tick (√) the appropriate features. Then answer the questions following the check-list. Finally, look at the pictures in this unit. Do you think the texts could refer to any of them? How?

Text 1 'Would you like to tell us how you feel about this new factory, Mrs Brown?'
'Yes, well as you can see, my cottage was in a wonderful spot before they built this thing here. Now I look out of the window and see smoke instead of mountains.'

Text 2 THE BIOLOGY DEPARTMENT WELCOMES:

Professor John Hawkins

Professor Hawkins will talk on Thursday evening on:

'Endangered Animals'

Main Lecture Theatre at 7.30 p.m.
Everyone welcome – no entrance fee.

The examiner may ask you more questions about the texts. Look at the questions below and discuss them in pairs or small groups.

Text 1:
How would you feel if you were the cottage owner?
What could Mrs Brown have done to try to stop the new factory being built?

Text 2:
What animals do you think Professor Hawkins might talk about?
Some of the things that have killed animals have been caused by people. Can you think of any examples of these?

Section 5 Listening

Listening task 1 Listen to two people on the cassette preparing a talk on pollution in inner cities. Look at the list of topics below and put a tick (√) by the ones they decide to include in the talk.

Topics
Statistics about the amount of carbon monoxide in the air
The growing number of cars in the inner city
Money from the council to help improve public transport in their city
Park and Ride schemes to cut down on the number of cars in the city
The need for more green areas in the city
Bicycle lanes to encourage the use of bicycles instead of cars
Making lorries in the inner city illegal
The need to make more pedestrian precincts for shoppers

Listening task 2 The Brown family are interested in going to the Gower Nature Park for their summer holiday this year. Listen to the answerphone service on the cassette and fill in the missing information below by writing short answers to the questions that Mrs Brown has written for herself. First read the advertisement.

> GOWER NATURE PARK
>
> Come and stay on the beautiful Gower
> Peninsula in the Gower Nature Park.
> Camping and Caravan Facilities.
> Open from June until October.
> Showers, toilets and washing facilities.
> All enquiries please phone:
> Swansea 24142 (24 hours for information)

1 When in June does it open?
2 How much will the car and caravan cost per night?
3 When is the reception open?
4 What facilities are there for children?
5 Is there an on-site shop?
6 How far away is the nearest town/village?
7 How do we get a booking form?
8 How do we pay?
9 Can I take the dog?

Section 6   Role play

Work in groups of three or four. Look at the roles below and choose one each. Before starting the discussion, work individually and read the information, making a few notes about what you are going to say. Try to use some of the new vocabulary you have learnt in this unit.

Role 1   You are a **factory owner** and employ a lot of people in the town. The town council wants you to buy some very expensive machinery to reduce the amount of chemical waste you produce. The workers have also asked for a pay rise or they will go on strike. Last year was not a very good financial year for you so you do not have enough money to do both and you really do not want the workers to go on strike as that would mean that production would stop.

Role 2   You are a **member of the town council**. The council wants the factory owner to buy expensive machinery to reduce the amount of chemical waste his/her factory produces. The local Green Party is very angry because the factory has not bought the machinery yet. Try to think of ways to help the member of the Green Party and the factory owner to come to an agreement.

Role 3   You are a **member of the local Green Party** and you think the factory in the town produces too much chemical waste – in fact you think that it produces an illegal amount. You know that the council has asked the factory owner to buy new machinery to reduce this pollution but the factory owner has not bought it yet. You and your group are planning to contact all the national newspapers soon to tell them about the factory. Think of reasons why the factory owner should buy the machinery.

Either:
Record the discussion on a cassette. When you have finished, listen to the recording and use the form on page xiv to assess your performance.
Or:
Choose one person in the group to act as examiner. The examiner's role is to stimulate the discussion if necessary, to make sure that everyone in the group has a chance to speak, etc. **and** to use the form on page xiv to assess the students' performance. At the end of the discussion the examiner should discuss the assessment with the group.

UNIT 6 | What's on?

Section 1 Vocabulary development

Use each of the following words **once** only in the sentences below:

> stage   screen   plot   acting   performance   row
> documentary   serial   play   channel   audience

1 Which (a) _____ is that programme on?

2 The (b) _____ was so small that all the actors could hardly fit on it.

3 We sat in the back (c) _____ of the cinema because we didn't want to

be too close to the (d) _____.

4 I think Shakespeare's best (e) _____ is 'Macbeth'.

5 'Are you enjoying that new (f) _____ on TV?'

'No, I missed the first two episodes, so I don't really know what's going

on.'

6 I thought the (g) _____ was superb in that film, especially Dustin

Hoffman's (h) _____ as the police inspector.

7 There was a fascinating (i) _____ about Eskimo life on TV last night.

8 At the end of the first act, the (j) _____ broke into applause.

9 I didn't enjoy the film much – I found the (k) _____ hard to follow.

▣ Section 2 Language focus

Look at the photograph opposite.

Exercise 1   Listen to the cassette. What expressions did the student use (a) with 'I', (b) with 'it', when she was **uncertain** about the information she was giving to the examiner?

Exercise 2   The student could not remember or did not know certain words or expressions, so she used different strategies to avoid them (e.g. by giving a definition or an explanation). Listen and write down what she said instead of each of the words or expressions in the list:

1 short-sighted	2 clean-shaven	3 in his thirties
4 properly	5 wrist	6 slippers

Section 3   Language application

Now look at the photograph on page 32.

Exercise 1   Make a list of five or six expressions of uncertainty starting with 'I' or 'it' which you could use when describing the photograph.

Exercise 2   Use a dictionary to find out the meaning of the following words:

1 cheering	2 staring	3 chatting
4 clapping	5 chewing	

Imagine that you can't remember these words and you need them in the examination. What other words and expressions can you think of to express the same concept?

Section 4   Text identification

Where would you expect to find these texts? Look at the check-list on page 81 and tick (√) the appropriate features. Then answer the questions following the check-list. Finally, look at the photographs in this unit. Do you think the texts could refer to them or any of the people shown? How?

Text 1   But for me, the best thing about it was Marta Roe's performance in the title role – she has made many films over the years, but there can't be many better than this one. Of course, having a director as good as the vastly experienced John Taylor is a big help. I wouldn't be at all surprised if she was nominated for an Oscar next February. In the meantime, I urge you all to go and see her – and it – at the earliest available opportunity.

Text 2   What do I like about it? Well, I think it's very well acted for a start – much better than most other soaps. You can really believe in the characters, they just seem like people next door, really, doing very normal, everyday things. The scripts are so good, of course, and some of the characters really make me laugh . . . that Mrs Johnson, for example, she's always got all sorts of problems but she always reacts in such a funny way! I must admit, I'm always impatient for Monday and Wednesday evenings to come round to see what's going to happen next.

The examiner may ask you more questions about the texts. Look at the questions below and discuss them in pairs or small groups.

Text 1:
What kinds of films do you like? Discuss a recent film that you enjoyed. What were the actors like? What made the film good?

Text 2:
Do you know any programmes like this? Which one(s)? What is the story about? Do you watch television much? What kinds of programme?

▣ Section 5   Listening

Listening task 1   On the cassette you will hear an extract from a radio programme giving information about forthcoming musical concerts. Put a tick (√) for each sentence below to say whether it is **true** or **false**.

	True	False
1 Claudio Abbado has never performed in London before.		
2 He has never conducted the Leipzig Symphony Orchestra before.		
3 There are two performances every day except on the first night.		
4 The box office doesn't close for lunch.		
5 The cheapest ticket available is £5.		
6 Bookings made by telephone must be paid for the same day		
7 Only certain credit cards are accepted.		
8 David Hawkins will lead the Boston Strings.		

Listening task 2   Listen to this telephone conversation between two friends planning to go to the cinema. You will hear **one** speaker only. When you hear numbers 1 to 5, fill in what you think the other speaker is saying at that point.

1 ....

2 ....

3 ....

4 ....

5 ....

Section 6   Problem solving

Imagine you are a Programme Controller for a television station. You have to plan an evening's programmes from 5 p.m. until 1 a.m. Look at the programmes below and choose the ones you think would make up the most balanced, interesting evening's entertainment for the public. What time would you put each programme on and why? How long would each programme last? When you have decided this, discuss your ideas with another student.

DISPATCHES

Ten years ago, Sayed Jaffar was a Birmingham schoolboy. He is now a local warlord commanding a 12,000-strong private army in Afghanistan and has a pivotal role in Afghan politics. He is an Ismaeli, a sub-sect of Shia Islam whose members answer to the Aga Khan.

INSIDE STORY   'The Psychic Tearoom.'

Fresh evidence that all Californians are barmy, in Philippa Walker's documentary on the latest craze for psychics. Star of the show is a Barbie Doll lookalike, Kebrina Kincade, who has looked into the future for ex-Philippines President Marcos, the Shah of Iran and President Sadat. Presumably she didn't have good news for any of them. Coming up fast on the inside is Sylvester Stallone's exotic mother, Jacqui, a mere astrologer. Her awful son disgraces himself by hanging up the phone on our girl from the BBC.

THE ERRAND BOY

(film, 1961): Jerry Lewis — you either love him or loathe him. For those of the former persuasion, 'Le Roi du Crazy' (as the high-brow French critics once crowned him) is found clowning around in a movie studio. He directs too.

SOB SISTERS

Even jokes about American Express raise obedient laughter from the studio audience. in this new sitcom about sisters thrown together by circumstances.

Concerning Cancer (Compass Films)

Writer and broadcaster John Morgan, a cancer sufferer, set out to make an objective film about the way cancer affects the victims and those around them. His original idea was to demystify the disease and dispel some fears and misconceptions. But as Morgan's own illness began to tighten its grip on his body, he himself became the subject of the film. The result is 'The Enemy Within' a film which is far from comforting as it shows Morgan's cancer to be as elusive and lethal as a guerilla sniper with incumbent assaults and retreats; victories, despair and finally surrender for the sufferer. Advances in medicine have made some forms of cancer, if caught early enough, either curable or at least capable of containment. Morgan believed he had acted on his own illness early enough to contain the disease, it wasn't to be the case. What the film tells us is simply that any attempts to explain the experience of cancer to a non-sufferer are futile and that every victim's disease is different.

LETTER TO BREZHNEV

(film, 1985): It appeared as one of those bright, fresh, finger-on-the-pulse movies, anticipating glasnost with its story of two latter-day Liver birds (Margi Clarke and Alexandra Pigg) who pick up a couple of Russian sailors (Peter Firth and Alfred Molina). It has all-round movie-cred, being low-budget, British and set in Liverpool.

UNDER THE SUN   :'Olongapo Rose.'

All nice girls love a sailor, especially the Filipino bar-girls working the strip outside the US naval base at Subic Bay. Occasionally one of them marries a serviceman and is immediately taken to the base's Bride School where she is instructed in the mysteries of washing machines, microwaves and other wifely appliances. For the rest it's a dreary round of fortnightly cervical smears and the risk of pregnancy followed by risky abortions.

Flying Squad

Explosive stuff tonight as the Sweeney Todd ambush a gang making a getaway after robbing a supermarket in Woolwich. Everyone is tooled up: one bandit is shot dead and both another robber and a copper are wounded. It was the crew's first day of filming — talk about baptism by fire.

Signals (Holmes Assoc)

Opera is booming in Britain but the public's growing enthusiasm isn't matched by the production of new works: the old favourites from Mozart, Puccini et al still reign supreme. 'Signals' contribution to this unsatisfactory state of affairs has been to back the ENO's search for new work by commissioning an eight-minute opera for television. The result, 'The Mathematics of a Kiss' by top playwright Anthony Minghella with music by popular composers John Lunn and Orlando Gough, is premiered on tonight's programme. Pity that kind of exposure couldn't have gone to some new young operatos.

The Nuclear Age

Part nine of this definitive documentary on life with The Bomb focuses on the Carter presidency. When he took office in 1977 he pledged to cut back military spending, to pursue a foreign policy based on human rights and to negotiate arms control with the Soviet Union. When he left office four years later he had ordered the Senate to halt ratification of Salt II and authorised the deployment of the MX and Cruise missiles. The programme explains how Carter's vision of a 'New World' crumbled under pressure from home and abroad and talks to former Secretary of State Cyrus Vance, Andrei Gromyko and the cheerful peanut farmer himself.

COMPOSING THE FUTURE

Celebrating the twentieth anniversary of the London Sinfonietta and the history of its most ambitious project to date, 'The Children's Crusade'.

THE FRENCH LIEUTENANT'S WOMAN

(film, 1981): The Harold Pinter season continues with his ingenious version of John Fowles's tricky novel — the Victorian affair counterpointed with the modern adultery of the couple cast in the movie-of-the-book. In retrospect, Meryl Streep and Jeremy Irons don't have much sexual chemistry. Karel Reisz directs, beautifully.

HORIZON   'The New Sixth Sense.'

A must for the well-equipped hypochondriac is the 'biosensor,' a neat device that monitors chemical changes in the body and interprets the information on a display screen or print-out. The implications for doctors, for industry and for people (such as diabetics) who must monitor their own health are explored by Jenny Hooper.

WILDLIFE ON ONE   'Parrot Fashion.'

The beauty, longevity and intelligence of parrots have made them desirable pets since earliest times (Alexander the Great kept them). But trade in the birds threatens their survival: 100,000 a year are believed to die in transit.

Midweek Sport Special

More soccer and more snooker. Nick Owen introduces highlights of the semi-finals of the Littlewoods Cup and Alan Parry commentates on the action of one of the second leg matches. Plus cue-wielding from Derby as the last quarter-final places are filled.

Q.E.D.

The second half of 'An Everyday Miracle' in which baby Darren undergoes a life-saving operation at the Brompton Hospital. His tiny body is packed with ice and a Spaghetti Junction of wires monitors his every function. His anxious parents bite their nails. If you like going 'ooh' and 'aah' and 'oh' and 'wow' this is the thing for you.

Wish You Were Here?

Trashy travel prog for people who have no intention of going anywhere except Benidorm or Butlins but tune in for the odd gratuitous flash of flesh. Tonight jowly Judith journeys to Zambia and crinkly Carter, who seems to have drawn the short straw, reports on family hols in Great Yarmouth.

Either:
Record the discussion on a cassette. When you have finished, listen to the recording and use the form on page xiv to assess your performance.
Or:
Choose one person in the group to act as examiner. The examiner's role is to stimulate the discussion if necessary, to make sure that everyone in the group has a chance to speak, etc. **and** to use the form on page xiv to assess the students' performance. At the end of the discussion the examiner should discuss the assessment with the group.

The height of fashion

Section 1 Vocabulary development

Exercise 1 Look at the drawings below and find the vocabulary for them in the wordfinder. Remember, you can use one letter more than once and the words can go in any direction in a straight line.

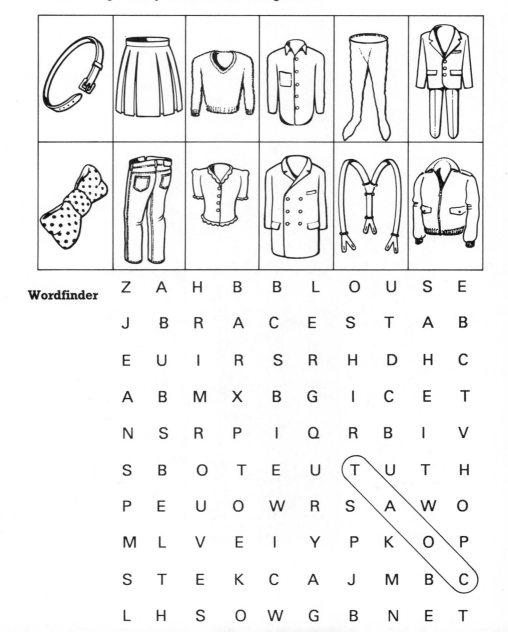

Wordfinder

```
Z  A  H  B  B  L  O  U  S  E
J  B  R  A  C  E  S  T  A  B
E  U  I  R  S  R  H  D  H  C
A  B  M  X  B  G  I  C  E  T
N  S  R  P  I  Q  R  B  I  V
S  B  O  T  E  U  T  U  T  H
P  E  U  O  W  R  S  A  W  O
M  L  V  E  I  Y  P  K  O  P
S  T  E  K  C  A  J  M  B  C
L  H  S  O  W  G  B  N  E  T
```

Exercise 2   Below is a selection of adjectives used to describe clothes. Make sure you understand them. Use a dictionary if necessary.

short   tight   plain   casual   long   formal   fashionable
smart   striped   patterned   dark   checked

Exercise 3   Work with a partner. Look at what he or she is wearing for thirty seconds. Think about the colour, pattern and style of clothes. Then turn your chairs around so you are sitting back to back. Take it in turns to describe what the other person is wearing.

Section 2   Language focus

Exercise 1   Look at the photographs below and listen to the candidate describing them on the cassette. Note down how many of the words (nouns and adjectives) he uses from Section 1.

Exercise 2   Now listen to the next part of the interview where the examiner asks the candidate which picture he prefers. Make a note of which photograph the candidate prefers and what language he uses to express his preference in clothes.

> Expressing preferences

Check your answers with the tapescript at the back of the book.

Section 3   Language application

Work in pairs. One of you takes the role of the examiner and the other the role of the candidate. Look at the photographs below. The candidate should first describe them and then talk about which one he/she prefers. The examiner should help by asking questions. Then change roles. If you can, record the interview and then listen to it and assess yourself using the self-assessment chart on page xiv.

Section 4   Text identification

Where would you expect to find these texts? Look at the check-list on page 81 and tick (√) the appropriate features. Then answer the questions following the check-list. Finally, look at the photographs in this unit. Do you think the texts could refer to them or any of the people shown? How.

Text 1   As I mentioned earlier in the programme, 'power dressing' mainly refers to how women dress. This concept deals with women who want high executive, high responsibility posts and feel that the way they dress helps to give the correct image for the job. For example, very feminine frilly blouses are replaced by plain ones worn with a dark, well cut suit in a classical style.

Text 2   Well, myself, I never take any notice of those fashion mags and all those skinny models who look great in everything they wear. Don't the writers of those things know that the majority of the population don't look like that and never will. Honestly, it makes me sick sometimes when you go into a shop and the assistant tries to sell you something that's fashionable and she says how 'modern' you look! What do they think we are – so blind that we can't see in the mirror how stupid we look?

The examiner may ask you more questions about the texts. Look at the questions below and discuss them in pairs or small groups.

Text 1:
Which of the photographs in this unit do you think is an example of a 'power dresser'? What do you think the person's job is?
Do you think that clothes give you a certain 'image'?

Text 2:
Do you buy any magazines – fashion or otherwise? Which ones?
Where would you recommend someone to go shopping for clothes in your town or city?

Section 5   Listening

Listening task 1   On the cassette you will hear the commentary of a fashion show which is for owners of boutiques who want to order their clothes for the summer. Listen and complete the notes on the next page for one of the shop owners who is interested in buying some clothes.

Summer Fashion Show

1 **Sunshine Dresses**

Style: sleeveless, short with a (1) _____ . Tight around the waist.

Material: (2) _____ cotton. (3) _____ colours and bright.

Price: 20 – £100   50 – £225   Individually – (4) _____ .

Delivery charge: (5) _____ .

Comments: Wait two months until May, then order twenty.

2 **Floral Blouses**

Style: short-sleeved, two (6) _____ , round collar and loose-fitting.

Material: 50% cotton   50% polyester   Flowery (7) _____ .

Price: 20 – £45   100 – (8) _____   Individually – £2.50.

Delivery charge: (9) _____ .

Comments: Very pretty. For all ages. Very popular last year. Order
          100 now.

3 **Lightweight Summer** (10) _____ (men)

Style: baggy jacket and trousers, (11) _____ style.

Material: cotton. No pattern, light (12) _____ .

Price: 10 – £225   25 – £600   Individually – (13) _____ .

Delivery charge: nothing.

Comments: Nice. Order half a dozen light brown suits. Might order
          more later if they sell well.

Listening task 2   In the listening test you have a short time to look at the examination paper before the cassette begins and a short time between the different parts of the paper. During this time, you should be preparing yourself for what you think you are going to hear. By looking at the questions on the paper you can often predict what type of information you will hear. It is very important that you use these short pauses to do this.

Below are the questions for a multiple-choice test. Look at them for thirty seconds and then close your books. Work in pairs and discuss what you already know about the subject of the text before you have even heard the cassette! Then listen and answer the multiple-choice questions.

1 The research for the book 'Fashion Images' was carried out by:
   (a) groups of postgraduate students.
   (b) Professor Brown and groups of postgraduate students.
   (c) the Head of Media Studies at Hull University.
   (d) Professor Brown.

2 The people studied in the survey were:
   (a) all ages under forty.
   (b) people who all wore the same type of clothes.
   (c) all employed.
   (d) sellers of fashion magazines.

3 During the survey, the people had to:
   (a) buy the same magazine for two years.
   (b) only buy different magazines to their normal ones.
   (c) only buy the clothes they saw in the magazines.
   (d) buy a different magazine during the second year.

4 During the second part of the survey, the magazine readers:
   (a) noticed they were changing their style of clothes.
   (b) immediately changed their style of clothes.
   (c) continued to buy the same clothes as during the first year.
   (d) gradually changed their style of clothes.

5 The main aim of the book is to:
   (a) show the variety of magazines and images presented.
   (b) make people more aware of the strength of these images.
   (c) help people who believe too strongly in these images.
   (d) help postgraduate students with their studies.

Section 6   Role play

Work in groups of three and each choose one of the roles below. Before you begin, read the information and make a few notes about what you are going to say.

Role 1   You are the son/daughter. You want to buy some new clothes that are very punk. All your friends are wearing them now and you want to too. The major problem is that they are expensive because they are made of leather and you don't have very much money. Usually, your parents give you some money towards your clothes.

Role 2   You are the mother. Your son/daughter wants to buy some punk clothes. You can remember when you were young that you had a similar problem with your parents. You can understand the position of your son/daughter but really don't want him/her to buy the clothes. You don't mind your child being fashionable but you don't want him/her to be punk. Try and reach a compromise.

Role 3   You are the father. Your son/daughter wants to buy some punk clothes. When you were young your parents bought all your clothes for you and you still believe that you, as a parent, should say what your child wears. You are worried about your son's/daughter's future as it will soon be time to look for a job. You don't like punks and are unhappy that your child has some punk friends.

Either:
Record the discussion on a cassette. When you have finished, listen to the recording and use the form on page xiv to assess your performance.
Or:
Choose one person in the group to act as examiner. The examiner's role is to stimulate the discussion if necessary, to make sure that everyone in the group has a chance to speak, etc. **and** to use the form on page xiv to assess the students' performance. At the end of the discussion the examiner should discuss the assessment with the group.

All work and no play

Section 1 Vocabulary development

Exercise 1 Look at these two sets of words. Do you know what they all mean? And can you say what the difference is between the words in each set? Work in pairs or small groups and discuss. Use a dictionary if necessary.

> pay   wage   income   salary   fee
>
> company   firm   factory   civil service   business

Exercise 2 Check that you understand the meaning of the words in the box.

freelance	overtime
	unemployed
badly-paid	full-time

Exercise 3 Then add fifteen more words that you associate with work/jobs. Write then in the box or on the blackboard.

Exercise 4 Work in pairs or small groups. Divide the words in the box into two groups. Decide on your criteria for the division and write the words in the columns below.

Column 1	Column 2

Exercise 5 Read your lists to the rest of the class and explain your criteria.

▣ Section 2   Language focus

Exercise 1   Work individually and list the positive and negative aspects of the two jobs shown in the photographs in the chart opposite. (Two examples are given.) Then compare your ideas with a partner's and add to your lists.

Cameraman		Office clerk	
+	−	+	−
In the open air			Routine

Exercise 2   On the cassette you will hear a group interview (the examiner and two candidates) based on these two photographs. Listen and add to your list any more points that they mention about the jobs.

Exercise 3   Listen again and notice the interaction between the three people: who speaks to whom. Does the examiner ask each candidate questions separately or do the candidates talk to each other? Listen and try to draw lines and arrows to show who speaks to whom. The first three have been done for you.

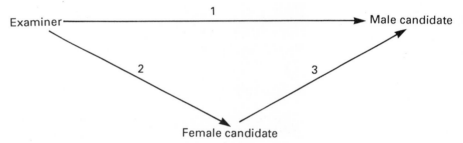

Section 3   Language application

Work in groups of three, one of you taking the part of the examiner and the other two taking the part of the candidates. Talk about the positive and negative aspects of your own job. (If you have not got a job think of one you would like to have.)

The examiner should start the conversation by asking what the jobs are. The candidates should then try to keep the conversation going. (Remember the interaction lines you drew in Section 2.)

Section 4   Text identification

Where would you expect to find these texts? Look at the check-list on page 81 and tick (√) the appropriate features. Then answer the questions following the check-list. Finally, look at the photographs in this unit. Do you think the texts could refer to them or any of the people shown? How?

Text 1   And now our job spot. An advertising agency in Croydon is looking for bright, ambitious school-leavers who have a flair for sales and marketing.

Good appearance and pleasant telephone voice are essential. They offer an excellent competitive salary and the chance to move up the promotion ladder fast if you are the right person. For more information phone 081-693 1294 right away.

Text 2 At present I am working as a supervisor in a large department store, a post which I have held for the last two years. I joined the company in 1986 as a senior sales assistant and in a very short time I was promoted to my present position.

My duties are to supervise a complete section with a staff of sixteen. I am responsible for the co-ordination of the staff and I have overall responsibility for the cash desks.

The examiner may ask you more questions about the texts. Look at the questions below and discuss them in pairs or small groups.

Text 1:
What exactly do you think the job involves?
Would you apply for this job? Why (not)?
Who do you think the writer/speaker is?

Text 2:
Would you like to have the writer's job? Why (not)?
What kind of education would you need for this job?
How old do you think the writer is? Why?

🔊 Section 5   Listening

Listening task 1 On the cassette you will hear Peter Walsh being interviewed for a job. Listen and choose the correct answer for each question.

1 How long has he been in his present job?
  (a) Since 1986.
  (b) For about three years.
  (c) For three months.

2 Why does he want a new job?
  (a) For a change.
  (b) To earn more money.
  (c) To get promotion.

3 What does he like most about his job?
  (a) The responsibility.
  (b) His colleagues.
  (c) Working conditions.

4 What kind of person are they looking for?
  (a) Someone prepared to work overtime.
  (b) Someone who is punctual.
  (c) Someone who wants to get on.

5 What qualifications does Peter have?
   (a) A degree.
   (b) A school leaving certificate.
   (c) A postgraduate diploma.

Listening task 2   Look at this advertisement for a job. Listen to Philip and Ann talking about the job and fill in the missing words.

An international (1) _____ import firm seeks a young junior

(2) _____ . Excellent basic salary with opportunities to increase

income through high sales (3) _____ . A company (4) _____ is

provided. Excellent prospects for ambitious young (5) _____ who

have drive and enthusiasm. The applicant must be prepared to

(6) _____ and must be able to work well in a (7) _____ . Interesting

and varied work. Apply in writing to the Personnel Manager, Eastern

Line Ltd, Harbour Lane, E4.

Section 6   Problem solving

Work in groups of three or four. First work individually and read the three job advertisements below and the personal information on the five people who are looking for a new job. Choose the best person for each job and think of your reasons. Then work together and try to reach an agreement.

SECRETARY

An interesting company is looking for a secretary to the General Sales Manager. The right applicant will have excellent typing and administrative skills and experience in a similar post. Good salary. Telephone 879387.

RECEPTIONIST

A small export firm requires a telephonist/receptionist. The post involves managing a busy switchboard and being first point of contact for visitors. Pleasant personality and good telephone voice essential. Some typing may be required. Experience preferred. Telephone 918765.

ADMINISTRATIVE ASSISTANT

Electronics firm require an administrative assistant to work in customers' accounts department. No experience necessary. Would suit school-leaver. Telephone 786543.

Name: Peter Williams

Address: 9, Crew Street, EC4
Education: 8 O levels, 2 A levels
One-year secretarial
course, Pitman's.
Previous work experience:
1983–5 shop assistant
1985–7 accounting clerk
1987–present assistant to
accountant

Name: Jane Casting

Address: 234, Bellamy Street, W9
Education: 7 O levels, 3 A levels
Previous work experience:
1987–8 typist
1988– typist and accounts
assistant

Name: Mike Potters

Address: 45, Hardcourt Lane, E24
Education: 5 O levels
Typing Diploma
Previous work experience:
1985–6 messenger
1986–present telephonist

Name: Gill Turnball

Address: 32, Broadway, SE23
Education: 3 O levels
Previous work experience:
1986–8 unemployed
1988– night receptionist in
hotel

Name: Lesley Neill

Address: Provence Street, E3
Education: 3 O levels
Previous work experience:
    1987–present hotel
                 receptionist

Either:
Record the discussion on a cassette. When you have finished, listen to the
recording and use the form on page xiv to assess your performance.
Or:
Choose one person in the group to act as examiner. The examiner's role is
to stimulate the discussion if necessary, to make sure that everyone in the
group has a chance to speak, etc, **and** to use the form on page xiv to
assess the students' performance. At the end of the discussion the
examiner should discuss the assessment with the group.

All creatures great and small

Section 1 Vocabulary development

Work in pairs. Match the words in the right-hand box with the animals you associate them with on the left. One example has been done for you.

1 sheep	A saddle
2 zebra	B prey
3 lion	C roar
4 cow	D farm
5 horse	E feather
6 fish**	F kennel
7 dog	G flock
8 canary	H cage
	I tank**
	J bark
	K stripe
	L wool
	M bleat
	N sing

Section 2 Language focus

Exercise 1   Imagine the examiner gives you the two photographs opposite to look at and to compare. What kinds of question do you think he/she would ask?
  What kind of language would you need to use to answer these questions? Make a list.

Exercise 2   Now listen to the cassette and check your predictions.

Exercise 3   Listen again and write down the expressions the student used to compare and contrast the two kinds of birds.

Exercise 4   How do you think the examiner would develop the discussion after this? What topic(s) would he/she be likely to ask you to talk about?

Section 3   Language application

Work in pairs. Look at these photographs of two animals.

Exercise 1   Compare and contrast the two animals using the language you noted in Section 2. Pay particular attention to the **surroundings** of the animals.

Exercise 2   How do you think the examiner would probably develop your conversation? What topics is he/she likely to ask you to discuss?

Section 4   Text identification

Where would you expect to find these texts? Look at the check-list on page 81 and tick (√) the appropriate features. Then answer the questions following the check-list. Finally, look at the photographs in this unit. Do you think the texts could refer to them?

Text 1   'Cruel? No, of course I don't think it's cruel; if I did, I wouldn't be working here! And I'm sure the thousands of visitors who come every year to see our animals don't think so, either. I think the animals have plenty of room to move around and get enough exercise, we feed them well and we are making bigger and better cages and enclosures all the time, especially for the larger animals. And don't forget the number of rare animals which have bred in captivity; without us, several species would probably be very close to extinction by now!'

Text 2   'Well, it's something that makes me really angry, it's absolutely disgusting! When I think about what the poor animals have to suffer in the name of science, just to try out some new product for humans, I mean, it's immoral! Animals have feelings, just like humans. Why should they be tortured like that? Why don't they ask for human volunteers, at least they can say no. Anyway, in answer to your question, yes, we will be taking much more action than in the past to put a stop to it.'

The examiner may ask you more questions about the texts. Look at the questions below and discuss them in pairs or small groups.

Text 1:
Which animals do you like to see in the zoo?
Would you like to work in a zoo? Why (not)?

Text 2:
Do you think experiments with animals are cruel?
Why are these experiments carried out? Can they be justified?

🖭 Section 5   Listening

Listening task 1   Listen to the cassette and fill in the blanks below.

The woman wants to buy a pet for her (1) _____.

(2) _____ eight million people in Britain have a dog.

Biscuits keep a dog's (3) _____ in good condition.

The shopowner expects a dog to cost about (4) _____ a month.

A dog licence now costs (5) _____ a year.

Dogs are more (6) _____ and (7) _____ than cats.

Cats are more (8) _____ than dogs.

Listening task 2   Listen to the doctor on the cassette and put a tick (√) in the appropriate column to say whether he thinks the following statements are **true** or **false**.

	True	False
1 Most snakes are not poisonous.		
2 Only two per cent of snakes are poisonous.		
3 Snakes never attack without provocation.		
4 The species of snake must be identified before the victim can be treated.		
5 The snake can only be identified by killing it.		
6 When a person is bitten by a snake, the only thing to do is to stop them from moving.		
7 The poison should not be sucked from a wound caused by snakebite.		

Section 6 Discussion

1   Look at the leaflet 'Good Behaviour' opposite. What are the problems of keeping a dog in the city? Do you think it is fair on the dog? Is it cruel to limit the dog's freedom? Discuss.

2   Read the brochures on page 56. What are the advantages and disadvantages of zoos? What about safari parks – are they a better idea than zoos? Why (not)? Discuss.

Either:
Record the discussion on a cassette. When you have finished, listen to the recording and use the form on page xiv to assess your performance.
Or:
Choose one person in the group to act as examiner. The examiner's role is to stimulate the discussion if necessary, to make sure that everyone in the group has a chance to speak, etc. **and** to use the form on page xiv to assess the students' performance. At the end of the discussion the examiner should discuss the assessment with the group.

Good behaviour

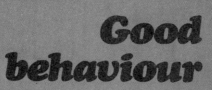

Remember that half the people in the country have chosen not to own a pet and probably don't want a share in yours. *Don't let your pet become a pest.*

*Start training your dog as soon as you get it. It's a good idea to join a local class. The most important instructions are: 'sit', 'come' and 'walk to heel'.

*Dogs should be trained from an early age not to wander, bark, snap or jump at people.

**Never* let your dog run free in the street. It could so easily cause an accident.

*Dogs should be trained not to foul pavements, paths or children's play areas. It is not difficult to teach them to relieve themselves in the gutter.

See one of the greatest zoos in the world
LONDON ZOO

See the animals

There are thousands of animals at London Zoo – waiting to meet you. See the two Giant Pandas, Ching-Ching and Chia-Chia, a gift to Britain from the People's Republic of China. See the sealions and other animals being fed. Walk through the world-famous Snowdon Aviary. Visit the apes and monkeys, the bears, the reptiles, and the fish. Drop in on the Moonlight World, where animals of the night are out and about when you come. From armadillo to zebra, there's always something new at London Zoo.

Have a great day out in the open
WHIPSNADE PARK ZOO

See the animals in the open

Come to Whipsnade and spend a spacious day in one of the most beautiful open zoos in the world. Hundreds of animals roam the 500-acre park, high on the Chilterns. Whipsnade is famous as a conservation centre for wild animals. Among the many rare animals born there you can see Przewalski's Wild Horses, Père David's Deer, cheetahs, and North American and European bison; Red Pandas too. There are also chimpanzees, elephants and Polar Bears. And, when picnicking, you may be joined by the peacocks and wallabies.

UNIT 10 | Dynasty!

Section 1 Vocabulary development

Exercise 1 There are many well-known television series that centre on the life of a family or group of families. Read the comments below by a student about two such programmes.

Dallas

'This is an American programme about the Ewing family who live in Dallas, Texas. The Ewings are very <u>wealthy</u> because they own big oil-wells. They all live together at Southfork in a <u>huge</u> house in the country. They are a kind of <u>clan</u> but they don't always <u>get on well together</u>. They're always having <u>quarrels</u> and <u>arguments</u> and they often <u>fall out with each other</u>. Then they make friends again till the next argument. I think most of them are really <u>selfish</u> and they aren't really <u>fond of each other</u>.'

EastEnders

'This is a British programme about a group of different families living in the East End of London. They are all <u>neighbours</u> and the programme is about their separate family lives and their lives together. None of the families is very <u>well-off</u> as this is a <u>working-class neighbourhood</u>. There are all kinds of families, from <u>extended</u> families with three generations all living together to one-parent families (<u>single parents</u>). A lot of the families <u>quarrel</u> and have arguments, but in general they <u>get on well together</u> and seem to <u>look after</u> each other.'

Exercise 2 Read the texts again and make sure you understand the words underlined. Work in small groups and help each other with the words you do not know, and then check with the teacher.

Exercise 3 Do you know any other television programmes like these. Work in small groups and write a paragraph about one of them using the texts above as models.

Exercise 4 Work in pairs and talk about your own family. How is your family different from the ones you have just read or written about?

▣ Section 2   Language focus

Exercise 1   Look at this photograph. Work in pairs and talk about what you think
family life was like for these people. Think about:
(a) the parents: what did they each do every day? Who did what?
(b) the grandmother: where did she live? What did she do all day?
(c) the girl: what did she do in her spare time/in the evening/at night/at the
weekend?
(d) their different attitudes to life and society, and their relationships to
each other.

Exercise 2 Now listen to the examiner and the candidate on the cassette and compare what they say with what you predicted in Exercise 1.

Exercise 3 When you talk about how people lived in the past you can use different tenses, for example:
(a) *the mother* stayed *at home and looked after the house and family.*
(b) *the children* used to play *in the garden at the weekends.*
(c) *relatives* would come *for tea on Sunday afternoon.*
Listen to the cassette again and notice how these tenses are used.

Exercise 4 Now look at this photograph. How has family life changed today? Listen to the cassette and fill in the blanks in these sentences.

1 The grandparents (a) _____ family. They often live in (b) _____ .

2 Society (c) _____ more liberal and children have more freedom.

3 Women (d) _____ more independent.

4 Men and women normally (e) _____ the housework.

5 The nuclear family has (f) _____ .

Section 3 Language application

Work in small groups of three or four students. Look back at the two photographs. Do they represent how family life has changed in your country since you were a child? Discuss how things have changed in your country and talk about some of the following points:
● the home itself: what it was/is like and who lived/lives there.
● work: which members of the family worked/work.

- housework, cooking, shopping: who did/does it.
- holidays and weekends.
- education.
- entertainment and spare-time activities.
- transport.
- rules and regulations in the home.

Section 4   Text identification

Where would you expect to find these texts? Look at the check-list on page 81 and tick (√) the appropriate features. Then answer the questions following the check-list. Finally, look at the photographs in this unit. Do you think the texts could refer to them or any of the people shown? How?

Text 1   I want to help my mother but I feel frustrated, helpless and angry. I know she's a widow and she's over 70, and it must be lonely and difficult for her to live alone. But she just refuses to go into an old people's home where she'd be properly looked after. She insists that she should come and live here with us. But I just couldn't have her here, and my husband doesn't want her here either. On the other hand, I feel so guilty about it. What can I do?

Text 2

Woman
It's a person who is different from a man. She cleans and cooks and does the shopping. She looks after me and other children. It's a person who shouts when I'm bad. It's a kind of person who wears different clothes from a man. And she is a different shape.

The examiner may ask you more questions about the texts. Look at the questions below and discuss them in pairs or small groups.

Text 1:
Who do you think is right: the mother or the daughter?
When you are old where would you like to live? Why?
Should the state help the old? How?

Text 2:
How old do you think this child is? Is it a boy or a girl?
Do you think a child today would write this? Why (not)?
How can we make sure children do not have sexist views of the world?

📼 Section 5 Listening

Listening task 1   Listen to Jane on the cassette talking about this picture of her family and fill in the information about the people shown.

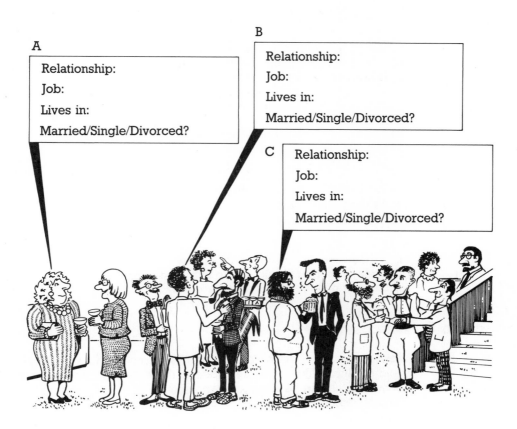

A

Relationship:

Job:

Lives in:

Married/Single/Divorced?

B

Relationship:

Job:

Lives in:

Married/Single/Divorced?

C

Relationship:

Job:

Lives in:

Married/Single/Divorced?

Listening task 2   Lesley and Mike are a married couple. They have just been to see a house for sale in the country. Read the following five sets of sentences. Then listen to the cassette and choose the correct sentence in each case.

1
(a) Mike enjoys gardening.
(b) Mike is bad at gardening.
(c) Mike is used to gardening every week.

2
(a) Lesley would like to live in the country.
(b) Lesley wouldn't consider living in the country.
(c) Lesley would prefer to live in the country.

3
(a) Mike thinks the price is very high.
(b) Mike thinks the price is very low.
(c) Mike thinks the price is quite high.

4
(a) Mike and Lesley have two children.
(b) Mike and Lesley would like to have children.
(c) Mike and Lesley don't want to have children.

5
(a) Lesley's mother lives with them now.
(b) Lesley's mother would like to live in the country.
(c) Lesley's mother lives near where they live now.

Section 6   Discussion

Work in groups of three or four students. Discuss what should be done to avoid situations like those described in these newspaper headlines. Talk about what should be done and who should do it. Before you start spend a few minutes making some notes on your ideas.

More and more teenagers admit taking drugs

Old age pensioner dies alone in his home with no food or heating

FAMILY WITH THREE KIDS HOMELESS – THEY COULDN'T PAY THE RENT!

Children die in fire at home while mother at work

DRAMATIC INCREASE IN JUVENILE DELINQUENCY

Either:
Record the discussion on a cassette. When you have finished, listen to the recording and use the form on page xiv to assess your performance.
Or:
Choose one person in the group to act as examiner. The examiner's role is to stimulate the discussion if necessary, to make sure that everyone in the group has a chance to speak, etc. **and** to use the form on page xiv to assess the students' performance. At the end of the discussion the examiner should discuss the assessment with the group.

UNIT 11

Getting away from it all

Section 1 Vocabulary development

Work in pairs and put the jumbled letters in the sentences below in the correct order. In each case the first letter has been underlined for you.

1 A town or village on the coast with a nice beach is called a holiday TORSER.
2 Before planning their holiday, many people go to a travel agency and look at several different REROCUHBS.
3 Many people love spending their holidays lying on a beach, SINGBUTHAN.
4 If you're going to a country where you don't speak the language, it's a good idea to buy a HASPRE OKOB to help you.
5 Many tourists like to buy SIRVENOUS of the country they are visiting, to give to their friends or keep for themselves.
6 Before going to a country where there is a risk of catching a disease, e.g. cholera, you should get a CONIACIVANT from your doctor.
7 Before visiting a country, many people go to their local bank and buy some RUNYCERC of that country.
8 The amount of another country's money that you can buy with your money depends on the CHAXGENE TEAR of the day.

Section 2 Language focus

Look at the two photographs below and opposite.

Exercise 1   Work in pairs and think about what questions you would expect the examiner to ask about them.

Exercise 2   The examiner, in fact, asks the student to compare and contrast the two forms of transport. Write down some examples of the kind of language you would need to do this. Use some of the following words and expressions:

The _____ is
{
a bit more
a lot more
much more
(much) less
} convenient/interesting than . . .

{
a bit
a lot
slightly
much
} faster/smaller/dearer than . . .

Exercise 3   Now listen to the cassette and check your predictions.

Section 3   Language application

Now look at the two photographs on the next page. Work in pairs or small groups and compare and contrast them in a similar way to the interview on the cassette. Try to use some of the following words and expressions:

I think the _____ is (much) more comfortable.

It must be very/more tiring to _____

The _____ would be less convenient than _____

I'm sure it costs less _____

You'd get there faster if you _____

You wouldn't have to worry about _____

On the other hand/However_____

(For language expressing preference, see also Unit 7 on 'The Height of Fashion.')

Section 4   Text identification

Where would you expect to find these texts? Look at the check-list on page 81 and tick (√) the appropriate features. Then answer the questions following the check-list. Finally, look at the photographs in this unit. Do you think the texts could refer to them? How?

Text 1 Day 5   Breakfast at hotel. Morning excursion to Villesia to visit the ruins, packed lunch to eat on the site. Return to hotel by 5 p.m. Evening free.

Day 6   Morning visit to archaeological museum. Lunch at hotel. Afternoon free. Evening: optional visit to local tavern for traditional dance display.

Text 2   'Listen, Mr Smith, we're really annoyed about this, your brochure was very misleading. It said the hotel had a beautiful view of the bay, and all we saw was a building site . . . they were starting to build a new hotel, and . . . the NOISE! What? Yes, yes, I realise that, but . . . Sorry? Your representative? Yes, we did see him once, but he didn't seem very helpful, or perhaps he just couldn't do anything about it. Anyway, we'd like to know what you intend to do about all this . . .'

The examiner may ask you more questions about the texts. Look at the questions below and discuss them in pairs or small groups.

Text 1:
Do you enjoy going on an organised holiday like the one in this text, or do you prefer going somewhere without making any plans or arrangements first? Give reasons for your choice.

Text 2:
Have you ever had a holiday like this? What went wrong? What problems did you have and how did you solve them? Do you think travel agents, and brochures, tell you the whole truth about a place?

🖭 Section 5   Listening

Listening task 1   Listen to a travel agent on the cassette discussing a holiday booking with two lady customers and then answer the questions below:

1 Customer 1's holidays will be from _____ to _____ July.
   Customer 2's holidays will be from _____ to _____ July.

2 Choose from the list of countries the ones which are mentioned in the dialogue and then match them up with the reason why the two customers didn't want to go there:

1 Yugoslavia	(a) There are too many old people.
2 Greek islands	(b) It would be too hot.
3 Greek mainland	(c) The beaches are dirty.
4 France	(d) There is no flight from London.
5 Portugal	(e) There is only self-catering.
6 Morocco	(f) It's too expensive.
7 Italy	(g) The dates don't suit them.
8 Spain	(h) There are no nice beaches.
	(i) They've been there before.
	(j) There aren't enough facilities.
	(k) There are only departures on Tuesdays.

Listening task 2   Listen to the extract on the cassette from a television travel programme and then mark the statements below **true** or **false**:

	True	False
1 Bhutan is a republic in the Himalayas.		
2 All EEC nationals need a visa to visit Guatemala.		
3 If you stay in Guatemala for 60 days, your tourist card will cost you $6.		
4 French passport holders must get a visa for Guatemala from their own consulate.		
5 A new limit of seven days will be imposed on tourist visas to visit Burma.		
6 Tourists arriving in Burma will not be allowed to visit the capital, Rangoon.		
7 At the moment, the only place you can obtain a visa to visit Burma is in Bangkok.		
8 Not all resorts on the Costa del Sol will be offering reductions for children next year.		

Section 6   Problem solving

First work individually and read the different holiday advertisements. Decide which holiday you would like to go on this year in August. Think of the various factors involved – time, weather, cost, type of holiday etc. Then form small groups and try to reach an agreement about where to go all together. Be prepared to give arguments for and against the different holidays and try to convince each other.

Either:
Record the discussion on a cassette. When you have finished, listen to the recording and use the form on page xiv to assess your performance.
Or:
Choose one person in the group to act as examiner. The examiner's role is to stimulate the discussion if necessary, to make sure that everyone in the group has a chance to speak, etc. **and** to use the form on page xiv to assess the students' performance. At the end of the discussion the examiner should discuss the assessment with the group.

UNIT 12
A time for celebration

Section 1 Vocabulary development

Exercise 1 Look at this list of words. Check what they mean by looking them up in a dictionary, or ask your teacher or another student. The photographs in Section 2 show some of the words on the list.

> mosque
>
> holly
>
> lamb
>
> prayer
>
> carol
>
> worship
>
> fir tree
>
> holy
>
> gift
>
> candle

Exercise 2 Work individually and try to learn all the words. Use any method you like to learn them – write them down, translate them, repeat them, etc.

Exercise 3 Cover up the list above and write down all the words you can remember.

Exercise 4 Work with some other students and talk about what you did to remember the words. Did you do any of these things?
- write them down
- write them down with their translations
- associate them with words in your language
- associate them with other words in English
- try to remember the sound
- try to remember what they look like
- repeat them in your head
- think of a context when you would use them
- build up a mental picture of the object and the word

📟 Section 2 Language focus

Exercise 1   The examiner normally uses the photographs to talk about:

1 what you can see in the photograph
2 topics suggested by the photograph

Imagine that you are the examiner. Look at these three photographs and make a list of all the questions you would ask.

Exercise 2   Now listen to the cassette of an examiner using these photographs to assess a candidate. Check how many questions you were able to anticipate and make a note of any that you had not thought of.

Exercise 3   Then listen again and notice what the candidate says. Most of his answers are very short. What more could he have said? Make notes and then compare with a partner.

Section 3   Language application

Now look at the photograph on page 74. Work in pairs, student A taking the part of the examiner and student B taking the part of the candidate. First, spend a few minutes individually preparing what you want to say – the examiner prepares the questions to ask and the candidate thinks of what he/she would/could talk about and the vocabulary needed. Then carry out the examination. When you have finished, change roles.

Section 4   Text identification

Where would you expect to find these texts? Look at the check-list on
page 81 and tick (√) the appropriate features. Then answer the questions
following the check-list. Finally, look at the photographs in this unit. Do you
think the texts could refer to them or any of the people shown? How?

Text 1   This is just to wish you the very best for
Christmas and the New Year. I hope
you have a wonderful time and may
1991 be a successful and happy year
for you.

Text 2   Well, I'm not sure I can promise everyone a white Christmas. There is a
low depression approaching from the west and this will bring cold
showers, sometimes of sleet and snow, to the north and north-west.
However, it will remain dry and sunny in southern regions, but rain will
spread from the north during the night, and tomorrow will be cloudy with
some showers.

The examiner may ask you more questions about the texts. Look at the
questions below and discuss them in pairs or small groups.

Text 1:
Do you send greeting cards on any special occasions? When?
Do you celebrate New Year? How?
What is your favourite festival or celebration?

Text 2:
Which country do you think this forecast refers to? Why?
Which season do you prefer? Why?
What is the weather likely to be like tomorrow?

📼 Section 5   Listening

Listening task 1   Jane wrote this postcard to her parents when she was on a Christmas holiday in the sun in the Canary Islands, but she confused some of the information. A few days after writing the card she phoned her parents. Listen to their conversation and correct the six mistakes she made in the postcard. Underline the mistakes and write the correct information. The first one has been done for you.

> Arrived here safely after an awful journey –
> we didn't get to the house till 5 p.m. The
> weather's wonderful – really hot and sunny.
> Went swimming on Monday and the day before
> we borrowed a car and went for a drive
> in the mountains. Will be staying for
> three weeks – am coming back on the 18th
> at 18.15. Can you meet me?
> John isn't feeling very well. I think it's heat,
> but I'm sure he'll get over it. And I've spent
> too long in the sun so I've burnt my arms!
> See you soon.   Love Jane.
>
> Mr and Mrs Jones
> 42 Peter Road
> London SW11

Listening task 2   David has been Christmas shopping and has bought these presents for his family. Listen to him talking to Anne about them and fill in the blanks with information about each present. Some of them have been done for you.

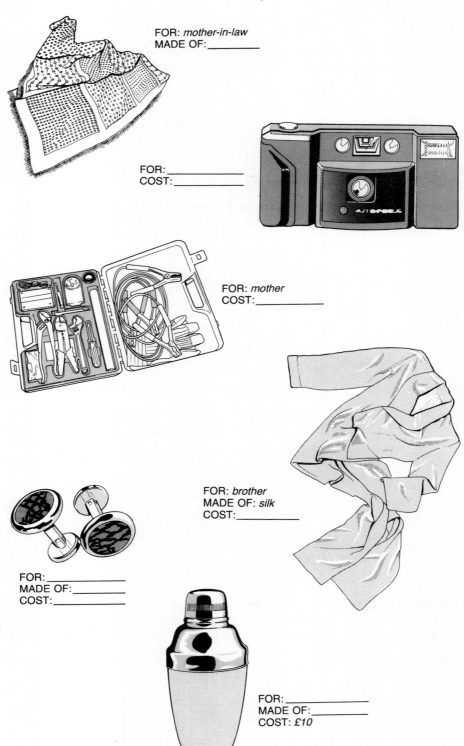

FOR: *mother-in-law*
MADE OF:_____

FOR:_____
COST:_____

FOR: *mother*
COST:_____

FOR: *brother*
MADE OF: *silk*
COST:_____

FOR:_____
MADE OF:_____
COST:_____

FOR:_____
MADE OF:_____
COST: *£10*

Section 6 Problem solving

Work in pairs or groups. Look at the two sets of photographs – one shows a variety of presents and the other shows people to whom the presents could be given. Discuss which present you would give to each person and try to reach an agreement.

Before you start the discussion, spend a few minutes making a note of the language you think you will need. Here are some structures to help you:

I'd give the gloves to . . .
I think the sports shoes would suit . . .
The socks would be better/best for . . .
The socks are too dull for . . .
I wouldn't give the gin to him.
I don't (really) agree.
That's a good idea.

Either:
Record the discussion on a cassette. When you have finished, listen to the recording and use the form on page xv to assess your performance.
Or:
Choose one person in the group to act as examiner. The examiner's role is to stimulate the discussion if necessary, to make sure that everyone in the group has a chance to speak, etc. **and** to use the form on page xv to assess the students' performance. At the end of the discussion the examiner should discuss the assessment with the group.

Student A picture for Unit 5 Section 3

Checklist and questions for section 4: Text identification

Checklist

		Text 1	Text 2
Mode			
Would it be written?			
Would it be spoken?			
Receiver			
Is it directed at	an individual?		
	a restricted group?		
	the public at large?		
Type of message			
Is it a	letter?		
	note?		
	advertisement?		
	conversation?		
	lecture/talk?		
	article?		
	announcement?		
	report?		
	extract from a book?		
Other (specify)			
Channel			
Would you hear/see it	on the radio/television?		
	in face-to-face conver-		
	sation? on a notice-board?		
	in a newspaper or book?		
	on the telephone?		
	in a note book?		
Other (specify)			
Would it be	typewritten?		
	handwritten?		
	printed?		

Questions

1 What is the purpose/aim of the speaker/writer?
(to threaten, to give information, to convince about something, to sell
something, to ask for advice, to complain about something, etc.)

2 What is the relationship between the speaker/writer and the receiver?
(friend, member of the family, acquaintance, stranger. Try to be specific,
e.g. father/child, teacher/pupil, etc.). How does this affect the language
used? (Is it formal, informal, colloquial, etc?)

3 What is the attitude of the speaker/writer? (aggressive, friendly, distant,
formal, hesitant, confident, etc.)

Student B picture for Unit 5 Section 3

Tapescripts

Unit 1

Section 2

Examiner:	Would you like to look at this picture of a classroom?
Candidate:	Yes. What an old school!
Examiner:	Yes, isn't it?
Candidate:	It's a very old-fashioned school. The students are all studying geography, I think, because there is a big map there. They all look very serious – I mean – I remember my geography classes and they were not serious like this. We used to go out a lot on trips.
Examiner:	You were lucky!
Candidate:	Yes ... er ... and when I was at school we didn't wear uniforms like this. These are so old-fashioned – I mean, we had to wear uniforms but not so old-fahsioned as this! And ... er ... I once had a very strict teacher like the one in the photo ... um ... he was my maths teacher (chuckle). And in my school the classes were mixed – girls and boys. In this picture I can only see boys.
Examiner:	Are you a student now?
Candidate:	Yes, but not at school. At the moment I'm studying law at university and it is very different to this picture ... well ... here the boys are not talking to each other and in my experience you can learn more when you discuss things with other students.

Section 5

Listening task 1

(Noise of people talking)

Good morning, good morning, everybody and welcome to our school. We hope you enjoy your summer course here with us for the month of July and I know some of you are going to stay here for two courses until the end of August. I hope this gives you plenty of time to explore the surrounding countryside and visit the many typical English country pubs we are lucky to have in this area (mumble of approval from students). For those of you here for one course, come to us for advice on which are the best places to ... um ... visit so you really benefit from your month's stay here.

By 'us' I mean myself, the twelve teachers that work here in the summer and, of course, the office staff. At the end of the day you will know who your class teacher is so I won't introduce them all individually now.

Well, before you go on your sightseeing tour of the area (mumble of excitement), I would just like to say a few things about the school. It has been open now for twenty years and during that time thousands of students have passed through our hands. I myself came here five years ago but Mr Franklin over there (mumble of recognition from Mr F.) has been here since the beginning so if any of you choose to do project work on ... er ... the history of the school, he is the man to talk to (chuckles).

The school itself consists of fourteen classrooms, a small study centre and a recently installed computer room which has proved to be very popular. The teachers' room is on the first floor and is open to you at all times, as is my office which is next to it. The building opens at nine o'clock in the morning so you have time to do your homework in the study centre before classes begin if you were out late the night before! (A few chuckles from students.) It also stays open until six in the evening so you are welcome to use any of the facilities after the classes finish at four o'clock. There is a rota whereby a teacher stays to help students with any problems (noises of approval).

As well as your classes here, there is a wide range of social activities that you can participate in if you like. This involves such things as horse riding, swimming and visits to local pubs in the evenings and day or weekend excursions to places of interest in and around this area (mumbles of approval from students). So . . . er . . . if you fancy trying a spot of hill walking or visiting the local mines, keep your eye on the social activities notice board. Our Social Secretary is John here (John says hello) and he will be coming around to your classrooms to let you know . . . um . . . what exactly is on offer this month. It is our policy to make your stay here as enjoyable as possible and because of this we strongly believe in an active social programme for our students.

Finally, on a more serious note, please remember that in the community you are representing the school. Over the years we have kept in close contact with many local groups and societies and some of our students have joined them for the period of their stay here with us. We would like to maintain this close relationship with local organisations so that our students can have the opportunity to see inside the life of a small community. So . . . um . . . keep this in mind when you are out and about, please.

And the last thing is a note from John saying that the start of the course disco will be on Friday night at eight-thirty (mumble of excitement from students). (John shouts out that it has had to be changed until half an hour later because the disc jockey can't come earlier.) OK . . . er . . . thanks, John. And let me just say once more – welcome to the school and England.

Listening task 2

Mr Hargreaves: Good evening, Mr Jameson. Please sit down.

Mr Jameson: Good evening. Now about my son Stephen's report . . .

Mr Hargreaves: Yes – just a minute. Yes, now – what class is he in? Oh yes, Four E – no, no, Four A, isn't it?

Mr Jameson: Yes, that's right. Has he improved this year, Mr Hargreaves?

Mr Hargreaves: Yes, I think overall, yes. Mind you, there is still room for more improvement in some subjects. Let's see – maths. Well, the major problem here seems to be his algebra. Apart from that he's doing much better. Could you help him with this, Mr Jameson?

Mr Jameson: Well – to be honest – it wasn't really my best subject at school either.

Mr Hargreaves: But the overall exam result was encouraging – sixty per cent.

Mr Jameson: Yes – and history. I seem to remember a bad report for this last year.

Mr Hargreaves: Well he lacks concentration in the class and of course this makes it difficult to remember things like dates and

	names and a memory is quite useful in a subject like this!
Mr Jameson:	Oh dear. Well, I'll have a word with him when I get home and see what we can do to improve that. And music?
Mr Hargreaves:	Music – yes. Is he still having guitar lessons?
Mr Jameson:	Yes, every Monday after school.
Mr Hargreaves:	His music teacher has commented that he doesn't seem to be taking them very seriously.
Mr Jameson:	I think it was just a craze he had, Mr Hargreaves. I've noticed that he hasn't been very interested in practising at home.
Mr Hargreaves:	And also he tends to talk a lot in class – I mean he's very talkative – and he only got forty per cent in the exam.
Mr Jameson:	Well, nobody in our family is very musical so I don't expect him to do very well.
Mr Hargreaves:	Looking at his geography result, though, there has been considerable improvement – sixty-four per cent.
Mr Jameson:	Yes, I remember him working at home a lot for some sort of project or something on – now where was it – India, I think, no . . . er . . . on China.
Mr Hargreaves:	Yes, yes – and it was an excellent piece of work – I saw it myself and was very impressed. And his Art classes have also been going better this year.
Mr Jameson:	Yes – he became very interested in 'Pop Art' after the school went to the local art gallery to see the pictures there – his bedroom wall is covered with posters from the shop!
Mr Hargreaves:	Yes, and fifty-eight per cent is not bad for his exam result considering how low it was last year. And now French. It seems that he has really taken to speaking a foreign language!
Mr Jameson:	We hoped he would because it's important to know another language these days, isn't it?
Mr Hargreaves:	Yes, quite.
Mr Jameson:	That's why we paid for him to go to France last Easter – so he could practise more.
Mr Hargreaves:	Well, it seems to have done the trick! Eighty per cent is a very good mark.
Mr Jameson:	Now, Mr Hargreaves, I'd just like to ask you one more thing about . . .

Unit 2

Section 2

Interviewer:	Would you like to describe what's happening in the picture?
Candidate:	It's a picture of a sports field . . . er . . . a sports competition.
Interviewer:	Uh huh.
Candidate:	And a, a, an event at that competition. It's a . . . what's it called? . . . um . . . a long jump, um, a and er it looks as though the girl is doing the long jump. It's a photograph of a girl who is in the middle of jumping. She has jumped and she is still in the air. She's coming down and trying to make the jump as long as possible.
Interviewer:	How do you know that?
Candidate:	Well, looking at the girl, I can see that she is stretching her arms and legs in front of her to reach as far as she can. And

she's wearing a number – ninety-four, I think – so it probably is a competition. She has a happy expression on her face. She is smiling, I think, and it looks as if she's confident. And there is a man sitting on the right. He might be the judge or he might be her trainer, he is wearing a shirt and tie so perhaps he is someone official. Perhaps he has to measure how far the competitors jump.

Section 5   Listening task 1

John: Well, what do we need for next week? We'd better think about what equipment Tommy and you will have to get.

Pam: What about you? Are you sure you've still got all your stuff? It's ages since you skied and your things must be really old now.

John: Oh, that doesn't matter. I don't need to be at the height of fashion.

Pam: Well, I don't think it's worth buying anything for Tommy. I mean, he mightn't even like it and it would be an awful waste of money. Jean's kids have all the equipment. Why don't we ask her to lend us what Tommy needs?

John: Yeah, we could ask them for skis and sticks for him. But boots are more difficult: they have to be exactly the right size so I think we should get those there – we can hire a pair on the slopes. It's not too expensive, especially compared to what they cost to buy.

Pam: Yeah, that sounds fine. Perhaps I could hire my stuff, too. What do you think?

John: Couldn't Jean let you have her skis and sticks?

Pam: Yes, I suppose so. But I don't like to ask her. You know what she's like. I actually think I'd prefer to hire them along with the boots.

John: No, listen. You can borrow my sister's skis and sticks. She's about your size. And we can get your boots along with Tommy's.

Pam: OK. And what about you?

John: Oh, I'll do. I've got everything I need. But we'll have to think about clothes. I've got my ski-suit from before, so I'm OK.

Pam: Jean'll lend me one of the kids' suits for Tommy and I've got my green anorak. I wouldn't want to buy anything especially just for a week.

John: What I'd like, though, is a good pair of gloves. You know how I feel the cold in my hands. I think I'll buy a pair for me and Tommy.

Pam: Don't bother for me. I've got the ones you bought me last year for Christmas.

Listening task 2

(radio)

And now the results of our survey on spare-time activities and sport. We wanted to know how people spend their spare time, so we interviewed women and men around the town during the whole of last week. Here's what we found out.

Only forty per cent of men interviewed claimed to do some kind of physical exercise while fifty per cent of the women we talked to said that they follow a regular programme of exercise. We also talked about watching sport on TV and both groups claimed to spend some time on this – forty-one per cent of men interviewed do this and thirty per cent of women.

We also wanted to find out exactly what form of exercise these people do, so we asked about different sports and activities. Jogging was by far the most popular with twenty per cent of men and eighteen per cent of women. Most of them do this during the week, either in the morning before going to work or in the evening after work.

Football was also popular with the men: thirteen per cent claimed to play, mainly at the weekend on Saturdays. Not surprisingly, none of the women claimed to play. Cricket was another popular sport among the men with nineteen per cent claiming to play. Again, no women mentioned this sport.

A lot of people also said they took some form of exercise other than these team sports. Eighty per cent of men and ninety per cent of women said they regularly walked as a form of exercise, either as part of their daily routine to get to work or at the weekends in their spare time.

Athletics was also mentioned, but not by many. Only ten per cent of men said they did this. None of the women we spoke to mentioned it at all.

Dancing was also mentioned as a form of exercise. Three per cent of men and women mentioned this. And also yoga. Five per cent of women said they did this regularly and two per cent of men.

Finally, a small number of people included gardening as a form of exercise. Eleven per cent of men said they did this and thirteen per cent of women.

Unit 3   Exercise 2

Section 2

Examiner: Would you like to describe the people you can see in this photograph?

Candidate: Well, yes, I can see – er – four people – two men and two women. One of the men is quite serious but the other looks more light-hearted 'cos he's smiling. He is fairly good-looking and his clothes are informal – I think he's wearing a T-shirt. The more serious man is very elegant – he's wearing a suit and tie but his clothes are a bit old-fashioned. Also, he is slightly bald.

Examiner: Yes . . . and the women?

Candidate: Well, one woman looks a little insecure – I mean, she looks like she has a lot of problems – maybe a bit pessimistic – you know.

Examiner: Yes, yes.

Candidate: And the other woman has got dark hair and is slim. She seems to be very confident. She looks very happy – I think she's a model or something . . .

Section 5

Listening task 1

Smith: Well, goodbye, Mr Johnson and thank you for coming. We'll be in touch within a few days.

Jones: Yes. Thank you. Goodbye.

(Door closes. Rustle of papers.)

Smith: Well – let's look through our notes, shall we?

Jones: Yes, yes – well, I thought Mr Johnson was a strong candidate for the job and he has got a very impressive curriculum vitae.

Smith: Yes, possibly too qualified, don't you think?

Jones: Well – it's not so much a question of *how* qualified he is but really what type of qualifications he has got. Look here he's . . .

Smith: Yes – I see what you mean but he's had a lot of experience in the retail business – two years as a sales assistant with this company and then two years here with . . .

Jones: Yes, but will he be suited to the post we're offering? After all, being a manager calls for different skills from his previous work experience.

Smith: Umm. He seemed very adaptable, though and that's the most important thing for the job.

Jones: Yes, of course. The sort of person I think we both have in mind for the post has to be flexible as they'll have to deal with a workforce of about twenty people. But there again, there are management courses to help train people to do this.

Smith: Yes, quite and I think that some sort of course within the first few weeks is a must for whoever we employ. We want someone who is interested in new ideas so they can keep us up to date. (chuckle).

Jones: Absolutely! Now – where are my notes? (rustle) Oh yes – have you got Mr Johnson's references from his present employer?

Smith: (rustle) Yes – here you are.

Jones: Umm. Generally a glowing reference though it does say that his punctuality could have been better at times.

Smith: Yes, but further on it does say that he wasn't a clock-watcher and was willing to put in extra time at the end of the day if necessary.

Jones: That's important – we don't want someone who isn't going to want to stay behind to sort things out if there is a problem.

Smith: I quite agree and his employer does say in his defence that he lives a long way from work and the traffic often holds him up in the mornings.

Jones: Well, that wouldn't be the case if he worked for us as he only lives ten minutes' walk away! Lucky him to be able to avoid the traffic jams.

Smith: Yes! Now – one thing he said about managers that interested me was . . . now where are my notes? – oh yes, here we are. Appearance, he thinks, is just as important as other qualities.

Jones: Yes, that's interesting. Being untidy is unacceptable, I agree, but I don't know if it is as important as, for example, being patient or reliable.

Smith: Well . . . er . . . yes – but I'm glad to see that we all agreed that being polite and tactful is of utmost importance.

Jones: Umm . . . but looking here at my notes he did say that you have to be firm too, but not so firm that the staff don't feel they can talk to you about problems – both personal and work ones. He thinks the manager's job involves helping staff in and outside work. An interesting thought, don't you think?

Smith: Umm, yes . . . well, what do you think?

Jones: Well, I think he's a good candidate but I'm still a little worried about a few things. Perhaps we could offer him a six-month trial period and see how things go.

Smith: I'm not so sure he'd accept – he's a married man with two children so he needs some security. But it is our policy to have this trial period for all our employees, isn't it?

Jones: Yes and there are some other good candidates among these applications – we could always look through them again if he decides against it.

Smith: Yes – we had a number of good applications but I do like Mr Johnson.

Jones: I'd like to clear up a few points before we decide to offer him the six-month trial period.

Smith: Yes – alright. Shall we ask Ms Brown to contact him this afternoon to arrange a time for him to come back?

Jones: Yes, now – when would it be convenient to see him? – let's see, tomorrow we've got the meeting for . . .

Listening task 2

Good morning viewers and welcome to the part of the programme where we look at your week ahead as seen in the stars.

1 Well – you sociable Aquarians out there are going to have a busy time this week, especially at home where family problems could take up a lot of your time. Make sure you aren't too short-tempered with your family as you could regret it later. Problems will begin to sort themselves out by the end of the week when your social life begins to flourish and you'll be the centre of attention in your circle of friends. Invitations will come from old friends who you haven't heard from for a long time and you'll find you'll be as popular as ever and you won't have a minute to yourself.

2 Pisceans, on the other hand, will find themselves with lots of spare time, just what they need after last week's ups and downs. You are usually a stable person but last week was a time of great stress. Use this time to keep in touch with friends abroad who you've not had time to write to recently. Treat yourself to some relaxing evenings at home in front of the television or at the local health centre in the sauna! This is a time for reflection: something that you pensive Pisceans love! You'll soon find yourself busy again, so make the most of it. Plan your next few weeks now while you have the time!

3 And as for Aries people. Well, you've got a lot of decisions to make next week concerning your personal life but this shouldn't be too much trouble for you decisive Aries people. Maybe things haven't been going very well lately and now's your chance to be more open and talk about them. You've been hiding too many emotions and they've made you unhappy. Your life has been dominated by jealousy and pride and it's time now to look back on your recent past and decide how you are going to improve things. You can't continue as you are as your friends are becoming impatient with you.

4 Moving on to Taureans – well – you are normally such organised people but this week will see a big change. Your routine will be upset by someone you are going to meet this week. This could be an old friend or a new one. There may be a trip this week away from home and you probably won't be making the trip alone. Saturn is in line with your planet and this means companionship so whoever goes with you will be someone special in your life. If this person is not special now, he or she will be by the end of the week! Only one warning – be careful of someone at work who could be too authoritarian for your liking this week. In general, a very sociable week spending time with people you like and meeting someone who could become important in the future.

Unit 4

Section 2

Part 1

Examiner: And how would you react in this situation? What would you do if this happened to you?

Candidate: Oh well, um, I think I'd be terrified. You know, I don't think I'd be a hero or anything. I'd give the man the money or whatever he wanted. I wouldn't try to resist or run away. I don't think I'd scream or shout for help – I'd be too frightened to do anything except give him what he wants. I mean, I think that's the best thing to do.

Examiner: Hum, um.

Candidate: He's got a knife, so it is very dangerous not to do what he wants. I mean, he's desperate – he might be a drug-addict and need money, so he's dangerous. The best thing is to give him the money because you can always get more money but not another life. Because, you know, this happened to me. A man with a knife stopped me very late one night – I was walking home – and I just gave him the money and he ran away. It happens often here and the police say you shouldn't put up any resistance.

Part 2

Examiner: And what should the police do to him? I mean, what do you think should happen to the man?

Candidate: Oh, I don't know. Well, first they should try to find him. If possible he should be arrested – but this is often quite difficult as he will run away before the police come. If they do arrest him, he should be put in prison, I think. Though, if he is a drug-addict perhaps he needs help. Yes, I think he ought to be helped in some way. Perhaps they should send him to a drug addiction centre so that he can give up drugs. And then they should help him find a job.

Section 5

Listening task 1

Police last night issued a description of two men they would like to interview in connection with a bank robbery which took place in West London last Friday morning. The first man is in his early twenties, about average height and build, with fairly short, curly hair, clean-shaven, eyes blue or green. He has a tattoo on his left forearm. He was last seen wearing an open-necked shirt and blue jeans. His companion is an older man, thought to be between thirty and thirty-five, with straight black hair, thinning on top, with a large forehead. Different witnesses say he had either a beard or a moustache, or both. He was wearing a light-coloured shirt and grey trousers, and his companion referred to him as 'Les' or 'Lest'. The public are advised not to approach these men if they see them, as they are believed to be dangerous, but to contact the police immediately on oh-eight-one seven-six-eight five-two-double-three, that's oh-eight-one seven-six-eight five-two-three-three.

Listening task 2

Policeman: Now Mr Wilson, we'd like to ask you a few questions about the robbery you witnessed the Tuesday before last, the fifteenth of September.

Witness: Oh, but I had an interview with one of your officers the day after.

Policeman: Yes, sir, I am aware of that, but there are still one or two little details we'd like to get absolutely clear, so if you don't mind...

Witness: Oh, not at all, I'm glad to help. What would you like to know?

Policeman: Well, sir, first of all we'd like to know the registration number of the Ford Fiesta. The number you gave us on the sixteenth was YEA six-one-oh J. Are you absolutely sure that was the correct registration?

Witness: Gosh, I can't remember the exact registration now. I mean, it *was* ten days ago... um... yes, I do remember those first three letters, they *were* YEA, because I remember thinking: that's easy, it almost looks like 'year', and I'm sure the last letter was J for Jimmy, that's my name, you know... but the numbers, well, I've no idea now, really...

Policeman: You see, Mr Wilson, we had another witness who told us the numbers were six-oh-one, not six-one-oh.

Witness: Oh, dear, um... all I can say is, I gave you the numbers that I thought I saw at the time...

Policeman: OK Mr Wilson, can you go over the events as you remember them?

Witness: Um I... I was on my way home from the chemist's, it was about twenty-five to six, I'd just bought some cough mixture for my little boy, and...

Policeman: How can you be sure about the time?

Witness: Well, I'd just been to the chemist's, as I say, and I remember saying to the girl, well, I suppose you must be glad the day's over, and she said, 'Oh, no, not today, we do normally shut at five-thirty but it's our late night tonight, unfortunately, we don't shut till a quarter to eight, so another two and a quarter hours to go!'

Policeman: So, it was five-thirty-five...

Witness: Yes, and just as I was going to cross the road, I saw two men run out of the pub opposite, jump into the red Ford Fiesta and drive off at top speed. There was a driver already in the car waiting for them, of course, so there were three of them altogether...

Policeman: Yes, and we found out that one of the barmen in the pub was the one who organised it all – he handed the money over to the two blokes who went into the pub.

Witness: Oh, so you've arrested them all now?

Policeman: All but one, sir. That's why your evidence could be crucial...
(fade)

Unit 5

Section 2

Examiner: Can you describe what you can see in the picture?

Candidate: Yes... well... there's a family here in the foreground having a picnic or something to eat, I think. But it's not a very nice place to eat!

Examiner: Why not?

Candidate: Well . . . here on the right is a factory and there's a lot of smoke. And in the middle there is a lorry and it looks like a very old one because there's a lot of . . . er . . . what is it?

Examiner: Exhaust fumes.

Candidate: Yes – exhaust fumes – it looks horrible! And here on the left there is a . . . . . . power station or something and there's a lot of smoke. I think that the sun is in the top left-hand corner but you can't see it because of all the pollution.

Examiner: Yes – it's horrible, isn't it?

Candidate: Umm . . . and here on the ground in the bottom right-hand corner there is a lot of litter – rubbish from the people who are having a picnic. It is a horrible place to eat – I'd prefer to go to the mountains that are in the background!

Examiner: Yes – I would too!

Section 5   Listening task 1

Pauline: Here's your coffee, John.

John: Thanks, Pauline. Now – shall we start thinking about this talk then? Let's see, it's on the 20th, isn't it?

Pauline: Yes, that's right. That gives us three weeks to plan it. Shall we start by thinking about what exactly we want to include?

John: Yes, that's a good idea. Now, here's some paper to make some notes.

Pauline: Right. Now, the talk is about pollution in the inner cities. We should include some information to show how polluted they are, shouldn't we?

John: Yes – it would be interesting to have some figures to show, for example, how much car exhaust fumes pollute the air – we could possibly get them from the Department of the Environment, couldn't we?

Pauline: Yes – then at least people would be aware just how serious this problem is! And then we could go on to point out where all this carbon monoxide comes from.

John: Umm . . . you mean, for instance, cars and lorries.

Pauline: Do we have any statistics about how much the number of cars in the inner city has grown?

John: Yes, yes – that's no problem. I think car owners should see just how much it has increased. People like to use their own car all the time, don't they?

Pauline: Yes – it's quite incredible really – especially as the bus service here where we live is not bad. I mean, in other cities the public transport system is terrible but at least the city council has given grants to improve it here.

John: Umm . . . but I still wish people would use it more. Should we mention ways of cutting down on the number of private cars by introducing, for example, a Park and Ride scheme so shoppers can leave their cars outside the city centre and travel in by bus?

Pauline: Yes – we could save that until the end of the talk as a possible solution. And how about the problem of the lack of parks and green areas – there aren't many here, are there?

John: No – that's a definite point to mention.

Pauline: OK – let's see – cars, parks . . . how about cycle lanes? They've been very successful in other places in reducing the number of cars in the inner city.

John: That may be asking for too much. We've been asked to write a leaflet about the subject too, so maybe we could include it in that instead.

Pauline: Yes – I suppose we can't ask for everything at once! But I really think we ought to say something about the lorries which are allowed to drive through the city centre.

John: You mean suggest an idea to reduce their numbers?

Pauline: That's not enough! We need the council to introduce a law to ban them altogether. I know the shopkeepers won't like it but . . .

John: Yes – it'll be difficult but it's necessary to make people aware of how much they pollute the air so let's make a note of that too . . . banning lorries in the city centre.

Pauline: (she starts to say this when John is talking about banning lorries in the city centre) Yes – and shoppers will feel safer with no lorries there. It's definitely time we had more pedestrian precincts too – should we include that?

John: I'm not sure – I'd rather keep this talk simple – the council won't like it if we make too many demands, will they?

Pauline: No, they won't. OK, well then – let's see. So far we've got these ideas – look at the number of . . .

Listening task 2

This is the Gower Nature Park answering service – thank you for calling. The Gower Nature Park is a privately run park on the beautiful Gower Peninsula in South Wales. It covers three hundred acres of undeveloped land and offers you a unique chance to camp and caravan in a picturesque unspoilt spot.

It is open from June the thirteenth until the last week in October. The cost for a tent is two pounds fifty per night and one pound for the car, and the cost for a caravan four pounds fifty and the charge for a car remains the same. There is space for thirty caravans and fifteen tents. The reception is open from seven-thirty in the morning until nine-fifteen at night for checking in and any enquiries you might have.

The park is easily accessible by car and to find out exactly how to get there just go to your nearest AA or RAC office and ask for details.

The on-site facilities include toilets, showers and a washing room equipped with washing machines and dryers. There is also a games room for children and a small social club where adults can enjoy a quiet drink in the evenings. In the camp-site shop you can get your daily milk, bread and fresh vegetables. The nearest supermarket is in Borough which is thirty kilometres away but there are some small shops in Townset which is fifteen kilometres away. You can also get petrol there.

If you are interested in spending your holiday with us on the Gower Peninsula and would like more information and a booking form, just telephone freephone two double oh eight four six and leave your name and address and we will forward you our leaflet with a booking form. All holidays must be paid for in advance by credit card as cheques and cash cannot be accepted.

Just one last thing – if you do decide to bring any pets with you, please keep them under control as there is a lot of wildlife living freely in the park. Thank you for calling.

Unit 6

Section 2

Examiner: Can you tell me something about the photo?

Candidate: Yes. Well . . . it seems to be a family . . . watching television. On the left, I think it is . . . the father, he's wearing glasses so perhaps he's . . . he can't see very well without them. Umm . . . he's shaved . . . he has no beard or moustache. He is in his . . . He is about thirty-five or so. On the right is his wife. On her . . . em, she is wearing a watch. I'm not sure but it could be a gold watch . . . and on the floor in front of them is their . . . em . . . it's not clear if it's a boy or a girl, I can't see the face . . . clearly, but I suppose it's a girl because her hair is very long. I would say she is about nine or ten. She's wearing something on her feet . . . not shoes, but . . . like shoes for the house. I'm sorry I can't remember the word. . .

Examiner: Yes, slippers.

Candidate: Oh yes, thank you.

Section 5

Listening task 1

Peter: . . . and that's the sports news for the moment. Now it's time to hear from our entertainment correspondent, Jim Weeks. Jim.

Jim: Thanks, Peter. Well, there's no shortage of things to do this week. Anyone who stays at home is going to miss out on some first-class entertainment! And perhaps the most exciting prospect of all is the return of Claudio Abbado to the Royal Albert Hall, to conduct the touring Leipzig Symphony Orchestra. Of course, Signor Abbado has always been associated with the London Symphony Orchestra or his own orchestra from Milan, so it will be interesting to see the result of this first ever collaboration with the east! They'll be playing Liszt and Mendelssohn. Starts next Tuesday at seven-thirty; matinees every day after that, in addition to the seven-thirty performance, until Saturday. The box office is open right now, and every day from nine-thirty in the morning straight through to six p.m. Tickets range from six pounds up to fifteen pounds, but it's half-price for students and senior citizens – that must be the best value in town! Phone bookings will be accepted but tickets must be collected and paid for within forty-eight hours. Please note that due to shortage of time, credit card bookings cannot be accepted for these concerts.

Elsewhere, at St Martin-in-the-Fields on Saturday, there's a visit by the American string quartet, Boston Strings, who'll be playing pieces by Schubert and Mozart amongst others, in a varied programme. Notice by the way that the leader of the group, Wayne Hawkins, is recovering from an operation on a finger, and will be replaced by his brother David. Amazing, isn't it, so much talent in one family – their cousin Rachel is also a noted pianist!

Well, we're not forgetting you rock fans. There's a busy week ahead, the highlight undoubtedly being the visit of U2 following their fabulously successful American tour. They'll be on . . . (fade out).

Listening task 2

Alan: Bob? Hi, it's Alan. How're things? (pause) Good, good. Listen, do you fancy going to the pictures tonight?

Bob: (1) ....

Alan: Well, I was thinking of going to see the new Woody Allen film. It should be really good.

Bob: (2) ....

Alan: Have you? Already? Gosh, you were quick. It's only been on four days. What did you think of it, then?

Bob: (3) ....

Alan: Didn't you? Oh, all the reviews say it's one of his best. I'm surprised. Hmm ... alright, let's go and see something else, then. Hang on a minute, I'll just get the paper and see what's on. Bob? Yes, umm ... what about 'The Chase' at the ABC?

Bob: (4) ....

Alan: Well, it's a thriller, I think. It says here 'The story of a police informer on the run from the Mafia's revenge. This one will keep you riveted to your seat!' Well (laughs) they always exaggerate a bit, but it's probably quite good. Harrison Ford's in it, so ...

Bob: (5) ....

Alan: Umm ... how about outside the ABC at ... well, it starts at eight thirty, so how about eight, that OK? Fine. See you then. Bye.

Unit 7
Section 2

Part 1

Examiner: Would you like to describe the photos you see here?

Candidate: Yes ... well ... here are four small photographs and they are all photos of models – well, they look like models, at least some of them.

Examiner: Yes, yes.

Candidate: Well – this one is quite punk! I mean her hair is. She's wearing some kind of jacket or blouse. And lots of bracelets and things. She's quite modern – fashionable – well they are all fashionable. This one is wearing very casual clothes – jeans and a striped jumper – very comfortable clothes. Well, these clothes here are comfortable too but they are quite formal. He's wearing a dark suit with a white striped shirt underneath. And a tie.

Examiner: Yes, and the last photo?

Candidate: Yes ... umm ... she's wearing a checked jacket ... it's short and ... er a plain tight skirt. She's also wearing a hat and a patterned scarf. She looks like a model.

Part 2

Examiner: What type of clothes do you prefer to wear? Do you like any of the clothes in the photos?

Candidate: Yes. I like these clothes best – the jeans and jumper. I prefer wearing casual clothes to more formal clothes because I feel more relaxed. And I like wearing jeans more than trousers because they are more comfortable.

Examiner: What about if you go to a formal party or something like that?

Candidate: Well, then I'd buy a suit or some clothes like this man here with the baggy trousers but only if I had to – I'd rather wear jeans than a suit but I don't think I would be able to!

Section 5 **Listening task 1**

Good evening ladies and gentlemen and welcome to our summer fashion show. We have arranged this evening especially for you retail buyers to help you decide on the summer stock for your shops. Don't forget that if you order now, there is no delivery charge but if you order later we have to charge you a flat rate of fifteen pounds wherever your shop is. So, for the best bargains, order now!

Our first item this evening is this sunshine dress that Susan is modelling for us. Now this comes in plain colours only and they're all bright to go with the sun we hope we're going to have this summer! (chuckle) They're a hundred per cent cotton so they'll keep you cool on those long summer days. The style is very simple – sleeveless, short and there's a belt around the waist to make it tight fitting to show off the results of all that dieting we do before summer! (chuckle) The price is five pounds fifty if you want to buy individually or a hundred pounds for twenty and fifty are two hundred and twenty-five pounds. Thank you, Susan.

Next we have Jane modelling one of our floral blouses range. These are designed for those warm summer evenings at home or abroad as they are loose-fitting to keep you cool. As you can see they're short-sleeved with two pockets at the front and a round collar. They're fifty per cent cotton and fifty per cent polyester so they machine wash easily and all the blouses have this flowery pattern and they come in various colours. They'll cost you two pounds fifty individually but if you order twenty it's forty-five pounds and a hundred and fifteen pounds for a hundred. And don't forget, order now and there's no delivery charge! Thank you, Jane.

And our third item this evening is modelled by Simon and it's our new range of lightweight summer suits for men. Again, designed to keep you cool with baggy trousers and a loose-fitting jacket. The style does not really fit those formal occasions – this is a more casual style for, I would say, drinks with friends in the evening. They are made of cotton and are all light colours with no pattern. Individually, they are thirty pounds – very good value for this summer – two hundred and twenty-five pounds for ten and six hundred pounds for twenty-five. Thank you, Simon.

And now we move on to our next item this evening – a summer skirt . . .

Listening task 2

Interviewer:	Well, tonight we have Professor Brown in the studio to talk about his recent book 'Fashion Images'. Good evening, Professor.
Professor:	Good evening and thank you for inviting me here this evening.
Interviewer:	Now, Professor, you are head of Media Studies at Hull University at present, aren't you?
Professor:	Yes, that's correct.
Interviewer:	And with groups of postgraduate students you researched into the fascinating topic of this book.
Professor:	Yes, yes . . .
Interviewer:	Well, perhaps you would like to tell us a little more about this research.
Professor:	Yes, certainly. I worked with groups of various students who helped me gather information and this was used, along with my own work, as a basis for my book. We spent two years monitoring readers of fashion magazines

in the Hull area to see how influenced they were by the images presented in various magazines.

Interviewer: Who exactly were these readers, Professor?

Professor: Well, we took a cross section of the population to represent both sexes and a variety of styles of clothes. We studied the 18 to 40 age range only as these are the people who the magazines concentrate on more than the, say, over forties. The only criterion really was that they had to be working – I mean that all the people in the survey had to be earning an income outside the home.

Interviewer: Yes and then what did you do?

Professor: Well . . . during the survey, which took two years, we asked these people to continue buying the fashion magazines they normally bought for one year and then change and buy a different magazine which concentrated on a different fashion style for the second year. Our aim was to see how much the images in the magazines they read affected what they actually bought in the shops.

Interviewer: And what did you find out?

Professor: Well, as expected, during the first year they continued to buy the same type of clothes as normal as they had not changed magazines yet, so there was no great surprise there.

Interviewer: And what happened during the second part of the survey when the people changed the magazines they read?

Professor: The results were – well, I can only say, extremely interesting.

Interviewer: Could you summarise what happened, Professor?

Professor: Of course, at the end of the second year we looked to see what types of clothes the reader had bought and then put the two years' clothes together. We found a tendency to change style about a third of the way through the second year and during the rest of the year most of our participants slowly changed their style of dressing without realising it themselves. It was only when we put their clothes from the past two years together that they could see there had been a change.

Interviewer: Did this change correspond to the type of image they had been seeing in the magazines during the second year?

Professor: Precisely – and they were surprised to see this change!

Interviewer: This example we have talked about is only one of many in your book, isn't it Professor?

Professor: Yes, I later went on to do other surveys with different groups of postgraduate students researching into similar topics which showed the power that magazines, images and advertising have over the reader. Most of the influence is subconscious and people are not aware of its effect on them, like the example I have explained, and some people's lives are taken over by these images and they hardly know who they are themselves. It is very important for the general public to realise just how strong this influence can be. My main aim in writing this book is to show just that. If I could, I'd like to explain another example of this.

Interviewer: Yes, please do.

Professor: Well, with another group of students . . .

Unit 8

Section 2

Examiner: Now, take a photograph each. Here's one for you and here's one for you. I want you to talk about the jobs these people do and what you think the good and bad things about the jobs are, the positive and negative aspects of each. First, what are the jobs? What's yours?

Male candidate: Well, he's got a camera. He's a cameraman. Perhaps he's making a film or working for TV.

Examiner: And what's yours?

Female candidate: Well, they're office workers. They're working in an office. It's a very different job from yours. Perhaps a negative aspect is that it's very routine. Yours is different.

Male candidate: Yes, mine is not routine. I think an advantage is that a cameraman works in different places and is always changing. I mean, there is lots of variety. And, of course it's very creative work. Not like yours.

Female candidate: Yes, but this can be interesting. And it's a very secure job. And you have a fixed timetable. A cameraman often has to work at all sorts of different times.

Male candidate: Yes, but that's not necessarily a negative point. It's part of the variety.

Examiner: Do you think the people in the office earn a lot of money?

Female candidate: Perhaps not as much as a cameraman. What do you think?

Male candidate: Yes, I think a cameraman earns a lot.

Section 5   Listening task 1

Mr Swaine: Please sit down, Mr Walsh. My name's John Swaine and I'm the personnel manager.

Peter: Hello. How do you do?

Mr Swaine: Now, this is just a short preliminary interview. I'd like to chat about your present job and what you've done up till now.

Peter: Yes, of course.

Mr Swaine: Well, could you tell me how long you've had your present position in Weston's. It is Weston's, isn't it?

Peter: Yes, that's right. Um, I'm not sure. Let's see. I left university in nineteen eighty-six – is that right? – yes, nineteen eighty-six. Then I was unemployed for about three months, and then I travelled round America for a few months, so yes, it must be about three years now in fact.

Mr Swaine: Um yes. And have you any particular reason for wanting to change jobs? I mean why do you want to move?

Peter: Well, I actually like my present job and still find it interesting and stimulating. The salary's OK so it's nothing to do with money, though you can always do with more. I suppose the thing is that I'm really very ambitious and keen to get promoted, so that's the real reason.

Mr Swaine: You say you like your job. Can you tell me what aspect you like most?

Peter: Oh dear. That's difficult. There are so many things. The other people are great, there's a good co-operative atmosphere, I mean, among the staff. And compared to other companies the conditions are great. I mean the office itself and the working conditions.

Mr Swaine: Um.

Peter: And then there's the fact that they give me lots of room for initiative and let me make decisions. You know, that's what I really like most about the job.

Mr Swaine: Yes, well, we're looking for someone like that. You know, someone who isn't a clock-watcher and who isn't too concerned about working fairly long hours.

Peter: Oh, I don't mind that. I'm used to it.

Mr Swaine: And what about your education? You went to Manchester University, didn't you?

Peter: Er yes. After leaving school I started a diploma course in design but I decided to give it up and did an Arts degree at university instead.

Mr Swaine: Good, and have you done any courses since? . . .

Listening task 2

Ann: Look. Here's one that might interest you.

Philip: What is it? Are you sure? The last one you sent me off to was a disaster.

Ann: Yes, look. It says they want a junior sales manager, and it looks like it's a big international company. That'd be good. You might get to travel.

Philip: What kind of company is it, though?

Ann: Um, let's see. Yes, it's a textile company that seems to import from abroad. That's odd, isn't it? What else? . . . They say the salary is really good. They operate a system of paying you a basic salary and then offering sales commission on top of that. They say it is high. And oh look! They give you a car to travel round in. Gosh! That's not bad, is it?

Philip: Um, do they say anything about experience?

Ann: Um, let's see. No, they want someone young with ambition and enthusiasm. Oh yes, they want graduates, so that's OK, you've been to university. Now what else? Let's see.

Philip: There must be some catch.

Ann: No, the only thing is you have to travel, but then that's what the company car's for. Oh, and you have to be able to get on well with other people 'cos it says you have to be good in a team.

Philip: Um, perhaps I'll have a closer look at that one.

Unit 9

Section 2

Examiner: Have a look at these two photographs for a moment. (pause) Now, I'd like you to compare and contrast them.

Candidate: Yes. Well, they are two birds, um . . . two kinds of birds, two

species. They are very different, of course. One is a domestic
bird, I think you say tame, it's a canary, I suppose it's a pet.
The other is a big, er ... large bird, like an eagle, but it isn't
an eagle. I don't know the word in English.

Examiner: A vulture.

Candidate: Oh yes, thank you, a vulture.

Examiner: What about the size of the birds?

Candidate: Well, obviously, there is a big difference. The ... vulture is
much bigger than the canary, and it is more powerful too.

Examiner: Which bird do you think is more popular with people?

Candidate: Well, the vulture is uglier than the canary, I think people don't
like this bird, it looks horrible. The canary is small and very
attractive, so the vulture is not as popular. People like having
a canary because they sing, they have a nice song. Vultures
do not sing, of course.

Examiner: What about the habitats of the birds? Where would you
normally see them?

Candidate: The canary is domestic. It lives in a cage, whereas a vulture is
wild and lives in ... isolated places, in the mountains, I think,
not near a city or town.

Examiner: Could you describe the appearance of the birds in more
detail?

Candidate: Well, these photos are in black-and-white but I know that
canaries are yellow. It's a nice, bright colour. The vulture in
this photo is dark, brown I suppose ... well, the body, the
wings, are brown but the head is white ... and the neck ... it
has a long neck, and a big ... er ... mouth. The wings are
very ... powerful. In contrast, the canary has a small head,
wings and mouth too.

Examiner: Do you know anything about the habits of these birds?

Candidate: Yes, I think vultures eat a lot of meat ... meat of dead animals,
I think when an animal is dying, they ... the vultures ... wait to
eat them. And they wait all together, in a group, I think. The
canary's habits are very different from this, it lives in a cage
and eats ... um

Examiner: Seeds, yes.

Candidate: And of course it eats a lot less than the vulture.

Section 5   Listening task 1

Customer: Oh, hello, I wonder if you could help me. I'd like to buy a
pet of some sort, but I've no idea what! Could you
recommend something?

Shopkeeper: Well, it depends very much on the circumstances, madam. Is
it for yourself, or ...

Customer: Oh no, it's not for me, it's for my little nephew, actually, he's
seven next week you see, and I thought ...

Shopkeeper: Ah, a little lad, yes, yes. Well, how about a dog? – they're still
the most popular pet in the country ... over eight million
people have got one, and they can't be wrong!

Customer: Oh, but I've heard they're very expensive to keep.

Shopkeeper: Oh no, not at all, you'd be surprised ... they don't eat nearly
as much as cats, in fact. Most dogs are quite happy with just
one full meal a day and a few little extras, like biscuits.

They're very important for their teeth, of course. And water, naturally they have to have a lot of water to drink – but that's free, isn't it? (laughs)

Customer: So how much do you think we'd have to spend a week?

Shopkeeper: Well, it's hard to give an exact figure, really, but I'd say ... I'd be very surprised if it was much more than five pounds.

Customer: That's per week?

Shopkeeper: Yes, a week.

Customer: What about a licence, how much would that be?

Shopkeeper: Well, until a few months ago they were ten pounds fifty a year but they put them up in the last budget, only by one pound fifty, though, so it's still very reasonable ... I mean, it's only a pound a month, isn't it?

Customer: Well, how do you think they compare with cats ... as pets, I mean.

Shopkeeper: Oh, that's a matter of individual taste, really. It depends what you go for, doesn't it? I would say that if you're after an affectionate, obedient animal, then you can't do better than a dog. On the other hand, many people like to see a bit of independence in their pets, so they would be more inclined to go for a cat.

Customer: Right, well, thank you very much for your help. I'll have a think about it and call in again sometime.

Shopkeeper: Pleasure, madam. Thank you for coming in. See you again.

Listening task 2

Interviewer: Dr Mays, we've had several reports this year already of people being bitten by snakes while on holiday abroad, and several listeners have phoned in to ask for some expert medical advice. So, what can a person do if they are bitten by a snake?

Doctor: Well, I think the first, essential thing really is to identify the snake. People tend to talk about 'snakes' collectively, when of course there are thousands of different species.

Interviewer: And which ones are the most dangerous?

Doctor: Well, I'll come to that in a moment, if I may. I'd like first of all to refute a couple of very commonly-held beliefs. Firstly, that most, or all, snakes are poisonous. The fact is that, of some twelve thousand species of snake known to man throughout the world, less than ten per cent are poisonous – and of that ten per cent, only a further two per cent carry toxic poisons which are fatal to humans. The second fallacy is that the snake is by nature an aggressive creature. This, with very few exceptions, is simply not borne out by the facts. Snakes have wonderful hearing, probably ten times more finely tuned than man's, and if they detect the approach of man will normally take evasive, defensive action –that is, slip into a hidey-hole or under a rock and simply avoid contact. The problem comes when the snake is startled and has no time to escape, for example when someone treads on them. Then, of course, the first reaction is to bite – but again, it's in self-defence, in nearly all cases.

Interviewer:	So you're saying that snakes will never make an unprovoked attack on humans?
Doctor:	Well, I couldn't be that categorical. It *is* very rare, but there is one species in Africa, the Green Mamba, which shows little fear of man and has been known to act in an aggressive manner without apparent provocation. But your chances of coming across one would be – oh, millions to one, it's not a common snake by any means.
Interviewer:	Well, thank goodness for that! (laughs)
Doctor:	But going back to your original question of what to do in an emergency – well, as I said, identification is essential, to see firstly if the snake is venomous, and secondly, what kind of venom it has if it is poisonous. Every poison has a different antidote, of course, and it's essential to treat the patient as fast as possible with the right serum.
Interviewer:	So how can identification be made?
Doctor:	The best way is to kill the snake, if possible, and take it to the nearest clinic or hospital, along with the victim, for immediate identification.
Interviewer:	And what can be done to help the victim?
Doctor:	Well, the victim must be kept quiet and immobile, that's essential, to prevent the spread of the poison, if any, in the bloodstream. A firm tourniquet, using a handkerchief or piece of cloth, should be applied around the infected area, for the same reason. But – and this is very important – the old housewives' tale about sucking out the poison from the wound, well, that can cause more trouble than it prevents, as it can affect the nerves around the injured area and set up a chain reaction, which will do the victim no good at all.

Unit 10

Section 2

Exercise 2

Examiner:	Now look at this photograph. It's quite an old one, isn't it? So life was probably quite different in those days. Let's talk about that. How, for example, do you think the parents lived?
Candidate:	Well, I think the husband probably went out to work and the wife stayed at home and looked after the house and family. I mean, she probably did all the cleaning and washing and did the shopping.
Examiner:	And what else can you say about the people and what their life was like?
Candidate:	Well, I suppose it was more normal for the family to stay together. For example, the grandparents would probably live with their children, and the children themselves would not leave home so early.
Examiner:	And what sort of things did children use to do?
Candidate:	Well, they didn't have all the things we have today. Perhaps they used to play more together instead of watching TV or going out. People didn't go out so much. You know, families were more united and relatives would visit each other more. And perhaps the families were more strict then.

Exercise 4 (same people talking as above)

Examiner: Now look at this photograph. It's very different from the other one, isn't it? Let's talk about how things have changed today.

Candidate: Well, there's no grandmother in this one. I think grandparents don't live with the family so much these days. They often live in old people's homes, I think. It's really quite sad. And what else . . . well, the children look different. I mean society has become more liberal and children have more freedom. I think that's a good thing.

Examiner: And what about women?

Candidate: Ah yes. Women have got more independent. You know, they live their own lives more. And when they are married they go on working so men and women normally share the housework. That's good, but perhaps the bad thing is that families do not stay together. You know, the nuclear family has disappeared.

Section 5   Listening task 1

Jane: Look at this one. This is a party my parents had a few years ago for someone's birthday, I think it was. It was all quite grand and they hired a waiter and everything – though just like my family, half of them got drunk.

John: Who's that? I mean the woman on the very left?

Jane: Oh, that's Aunt Agnes. She's my mother's sister. She got married very young and has three grown-up children now who have all left home. She's great fun and she and I get on really well. She says she's old-fashioned and doesn't know anything about the world 'cos she's always been a housewife, but in fact she's really very broadminded about most things. The woman she's talking to is a neighbour, I think. They're great friends 'cos they both have three children about the same age. The neighbour's a housewife too, I think.

John: And who's that man?

Jane: The one with his back to the camera?

John: Yes, in the middle of the two other men.

Jane: Oh, that's her husband, Uncle Arthur. He's OK, but he can be a bit of a bore. He's a bank manager, so I suppose that's why. They live up north in Manchester now. The man on the right is a colleague of his. He's also a bank manager, but he lives in London. Now, let's see . . . who else is there? The man in the middle of the group on the right is my cousin. He's a teacher and he's really pompous and full of himself. Thank goodness he lives up in Scotland. And do you see that chap with the long hair and the beard over to the right . . .? He's wearing glasses.

John: Oh yes.

Jane: Well, he's another uncle, but on my father's side. He's one of the odd ones in the family. He married someone really weird but it didn't work out and they ended up in the divorce courts after only a year. He's a freelance designer and has a bohemian kind of life in Paris. We hardly ever see him. He's talking to a friend of my father's. I can't remember his name.

Listening task 2

Mike: Well, that was a nice drive. I must say, it does make a difference getting out of the city. I feel just like I've been on holiday.

Lesley: Um, we've been stuck in the car for an hour and a half. Some holiday!

Mike: Oh, come on, Lesley. Just think of that house. It's much bigger than this one – and all that space in the garden. Can you imagine?

Lesley: And who'd look after it?

Mike: I would. I used to work a lot in the garden when I lived at home with my parents and my father was alive, and I really like it. And I wasn't bad at it, I can tell you.

Lesley: Well, I wouldn't even dream of going to live in the country, even if you paid me to. I've always lived in the city and that's what I'm used to. And you have too, so I don't know why this sudden urge to move.

Mike: 'Cos it makes sense, that's why. Money sense. Houses here are worth a fortune these days. Why, that place we saw was a real bargain in comparison.

Lesley: No, it wasn't. It costs more than this house. The price is much higher.

Mike: Well, quite, but that's because prices have gone up all round recently. I tell you, it's a give-away, a real bargain. And just look at all that extra space.

Lesley: What do we want more space for? We're hardly the average two child family unit.

Mike: Heaven forbid! Don't you go changing your mind about having kids. We're OK as we are.

Lesley: Don't worry. I'm not into washing nappies and sleepless nights either. But now that we're thinking of space, it would be handy for my mother. I mean, she could move in with us.

Mike: What do you mean? She's hardly ever out of the house as it is – and she's got her own house just round the corner. What would it be like if she actually lived with us? She'd never give us a minute on our own.

Lesley: Now, now, Mike. She is my mother. And I was only saying if we had the space . . .

Unit 11

Section 2

Examiner: Now I'd like you to look at these two photographs and compare them.

Candidate: Yes, I can see a plane and a train. They are two very different ways of travelling.

Examiner: Which one do you prefer?

Candidate: Well, I think it depends on the moment or on the . . . circumstances. The plane is the fastest way to travel, of course, and it's very comfortable, too. So . . . um . . . if I have, no, if I am in a hurry, I would prefer the plane. Yes, it's faster and more comfortable than a train.

Examiner: No disadvantages of the plane?

Candidate: Oh yes, I think perhaps it's more dangerous to go by plane, you know, sometimes there are accidents, recently we saw that a plane er . . . that there was a plane crash, and everybody was killed. Of course sometimes there is a train crash too, but I think generally it's not so serious . . . um . . . not so many people are killed.

Examiner: Mmm. Any other disadvantages of the plane?

Candidate: I think it can be very expensive to fly . . . it certainly costs more than the train, so if it's only a short distance, maybe it would be better to go by train. And I think perhaps some people are afraid . . . um . . . more afraid when they fly.

Examiner: Alright, what about the train? Apart from cost and safety, do you think the train has any other advantages?

Candidate: Well, um . . . you can see the countryside if you go by train, so it's more interesting for some people than flying. And also you can move around if you want to, there is more room than on a plane.

Section 5   Listening task 1

Travel Agent: Good morning, can I help you?

Customer 1: Yes, good morning. We'd like to book a holiday for July, please.

Travel Agent: Certainly. Where did you have in mind?

Customer 1: Oh, well, we haven't thought a lot about it, really. We'd just like to go somewhere hot, you know, and it must be in July.

Travel Agent: I see. Well, let's get the dates cleared up first, then we can see about availability. What part of July were you thinking of?

Customer 2: Ah, well, you see, we have slightly different holidays. I've got the whole month except for the last four days, so I could go from the first to the twenty-seventh, but my friend here doesn't start until the seventh, so I suppose it will have to be the middle two weeks, really.

Customer 1: Yes, but I've got to be back by the twenty-fourth.

Travel Agent: OK. Now, let's find a destination. Any preferences . . . Spain, Greece, Portugal . . .?

Customer 1: Oh, not Spain, we went there last year and it was absolutely packed with teenagers making noise and getting drunk all the time.

Customer 2: Yes, it was terrible. We definitely want somewhere quieter this year.

Travel Agent: Well, of course it depends more on the resort, rather than the country. There are resorts in every country which cater for the family or the slightly older person . . . they're usually a shade more expensive, though, as you might expect.

Customer 1: Oh, well we don't mind paying a bit more if it means more peace and quiet, do we?

Customer 2: Definitely not, it'd be well worth it!

Travel Agent: Alright, let's have a look at what we've got on the computer. (pause) July . . . was it ten or fourteen nights you wanted?

Customer 1: Oh, the fortnight, please.

Travel Agent: Right . . . well, let's start with Italy. Umm, we've got fourteen nights bed and breakfast in Sorrento for three hundred and

	forty-five pounds, from Manchester, on the fourteenth, or we've got . . .
Customer 1:	No, wait a minute, that's no good for me, we wouldn't get back till the twenty-eighth, and I've got to be back at work before that.
Travel Agent:	Oh yes. Umm . . . how about Opatija, two weeks half-board . . .
Customer 2:	Where's that?
Travel Agent:	Yugoslavia, madam. Northern part. Nice little place. That would be three hundred and ten pounds, from Manchester again.
Customer 1:	Yugoslavia? Oh, but I've been told the beaches aren't very nice there.
Travel Agent:	Well, again it depends where you go. In Opatija, they have those big wooden platforms, you know, with sunbeds, so there's no beach as such, but the water is beautifully clean and . . .
Customer 2:	Oh, no, I think we'd prefer a real beach, you know, I like a bit of sand . . . (laughs)
Travel Agent:	Alright, how about Greece, the Greek islands? We have several holidays available there, Spetse, Kos . . . Departures every Tuesday, and it's quite economical really because it's all on a self-catering basis, so . . .
Customer 1:	Oh, what about hotels, we'd prefer to be in a nice hotel, I think. What about you, Kath?
Customer 2:	Oh yes, I can't be bothered with cooking your own meals and all that sort of thing . . . I like to forget about all that when I go on holiday.
Travel Agent:	Hummm. Well, I'm afraid it's all self-catering we do for the Greek islands. How about the mainland? There's a dual-centre holiday here, Athens and Delphi, seven days in each. That would come to . . .
Customer 2:	Oh, just a minute, isn't it a bit sweltering in Athens at that time of year?
Travel Agent:	Well, it's not exactly the coldest place in Europe, no. (laughs) Let's see . . . the average temperature in July is . . . twenty-nine centigrade, that's eighty-one fahrenheit.
Customer 1:	Oh God, no, I think we'd just die in all that heat, I mean, the coast's bad enough but in a city . . .!
Travel Agent:	All right, let's try somewhere else. How about Portugal?
Customer 2:	Oh, that sounds great. (to friend) We've never been there, have we?
Travel Agent:	Let's see now. We've got fourteen nights in Albufeira, half-board, from Gatwick, for three hundred and eighty-five pounds.
Customer 1:	Albufeira? Oh, wait a minute, did you say the flight was from London?
Travel Agent:	That's right, from Gatwick.
Customer 1:	Oh well, really we'd prefer a flight from the North somewhere, Manchester perhaps or even Glasgow . . .
Travel Agent:	Right . . . there's a twelve-night holiday in Lagos, that's near Albufeira, from Manchester on the eleventh, for . . . four

hundred and fifty-five pounds.

Customer 2: Oh, that's a bit pricey, isn't it? Why is it so much more than the other one?

Travel Agent: Well, madam, there's a surcharge for the airport, and it *is* a five-star hotel.

Customer 2: Oh, well it's a bit over our budget, really . . .

Listening task 2

'Hello and welcome to another edition of "Your Holiday". And in tonight's programme, we'll have reports on Sardinia, Austria, the Black Sea coast of Turkey and the little-known kingdom of Bhutan, way up in the Himalayas. But first we go over to our news desk and Chris Wells. Chris . . .'

'Thanks, Mary. And first of all, some up-to-date news for potential visitors to Guatemala, as there has been some confusion about who needs a visa and who needs a tourist card. Well, if you're travelling on a British or Irish passport, you'll have to shell out ten dollars for a visa, which is valid for a stay of up to thirty days, and must be obtained before travelling to Guatemala. Apparently, visa extensions are very difficult to obtain. Most other EEC nationals can obtain a tourist card on arrival at the border for just one dollar, valid for thirty days extendable to ninety, but this extension will cost you a further five dollars. At the moment, it is unclear if this applies to French nationals, who may need a visa – check at your local consulate before leaving for Guatemala.

'Switching to Asia now, and Burma has announced that the tourist visa facility will not be available for the time being. Regular viewers of this programme will no doubt remember that visas were always restricted to seven days in any case, but apparently you won't even get your week in now. The reason given is the recent spate of unrest within the country, particularly in and around the capital, Rangoon, where visitors' safety cannot be guaranteed at present. Now, we have had reports from our correspondent in Thailand that the Burmese Embassy in Bangkok is continuing to issue seven-day visas despite the official announcement, but it would seem a risky business going there at the moment, even if you can get in.

'And finally from me, news of a welcome price reduction for children under the age of five at most resorts on the Costa del Sol in the south of Spain – there'll be at least twenty-five per cent off all year round, and as much as seventy per cent off in the low season, depending on the resorts. And on that happy note, it's back to you, Mary.'

Unit 12

Section 2

Examiner: Now look at the first photograph. What can you see?

Candidate: Well, there's a Christmas tree. It's in a house.

Examiner: Yes, and what time of year is it? When is it?

Candidate: It's Christmas.

Examiner: Why is the tree decorated?

Candidate: It's a custom in England and other countries.

Examiner: OK and what about picture two? What can you see there?

Candidate: Er . . . a religious ceremony of some sort.

Examiner: And where is it?

Candidate: In Greece.

Examiner: OK and who can you see?

Candidate: Well, some people and, er, a priest, a Greek priest.
Examiner: Yes, now look at photograph three. What is the boy doing?
Candidate: He's washing himself, his feet and his face.
Examiner: Do you know why?
Candidate: Well, I think it's a Moslem custom before praying.

Section 5   Listening task 1

(Telephone conversation)

Jane: Hi, mum. How are things?
Mother: Oh, hello, Jane. Are you alright?
Jane: Yeah, great! I just thought I'd phone to let you know we're OK. It's all really wonderful. The weather's fantastic. I'm sitting here in short sleeves and I'm still hot. I can't believe it's December.
Mother: Lucky you! It's like Siberia here. We've got the heating going full blast tonight. It seems funny that it could be hot anywhere else.
Jane: Did you get my card?
Mother: No, the postman hasn't been for a couple of days. But you know what the post's like at this time of the year. They've probably got a back-log to catch up on. How was your flight in the end, by the way?
Jane: Ugh. Awful! It was a typical charter. We were delayed and had to sit around for hours so we didn't take off till after midnight and it was five in the morning before we got to the hotel.
Mother: Oh dear. What a pity.
Jane: But we're making up for it now. On Monday we had a great day on the beach just lying around in the sun and swimming – the water's lovely, you know. Not at all cold. That was to recover from Sunday when we hired a car from one of those rent-a-car agencies and drove all round the island, up into the mountains. It was really spectacular. I mean, the scenery is wonderful.
Mother: Oh, that's good. I can see you're going to have a good fortnight.
Jane: Yeah, it's all going by too fast. A fortnight is too short. I wish now we'd booked three weeks instead. Still, can't be helped. Listen, do you think you could come and meet us when we get back? The plane gets in at about six fifteen on the eighth. Let's see, I have the ticket here. Yes, it says 'Arrive six fifteen on January the eighth'.
Mother: Yes, of course, dear. Don't worry, we'll be there. Now just make sure you put lots of cream on if you're lying in the sun in all that heat.
Jane: Well actually I fell asleep on the beach the other day and have a really red nose – all peeling and burnt.
Mother: Well, be careful. And what's John up to?
Jane: Oh, he's having a lie down. He isn't feeling very well today. I think it's something he ate. We had a big meal out last night so perhaps the food was too heavy. You know they eat really late here. We have still another hour before dinner.
Mother: Good heavens. We had our supper two hours ago . . . (fade)

Listening task 2

Anne: Well, come on then. Let's see what you've bought.
David: Let me get my coat off first. What a day! The shops are packed

and trying to get served is murder. I got most of what I wanted, but I think I'll have to go back up another day for a few more odds and ends.

Anne: What is this? A camera?

David: Yes, I got it for my sister's boyfriend. They're always going off at the weekends birdwatching, and they were saying the other day that they needed a new one. It was incredibly expensive. It put me back thirty pounds fifty. Can you imagine?

Anne: Gosh, those cuff-links are nice. Are they real gold?

David: Good heavens, no! They're only metal and leather. I thought I'd give them to my father-in-law. He's the only one I know who actually wears cuff-links these days. I thought they were quite a bargain – only thirteen pounds sixty.

Anne: Um, yes. That cocktail shaker looks nice. It's not silver, is it?

David: No, 'fraid not. Just metal. I got it for my doctor.

Anne: Your doctor?

David: Yes, I always give her something. It's a tradition. It was quite cheap. Only ten quid.

Anne: What else have you got, then?

David: Well, I found this really nice scarf. You'd like it.

Anne: Oh, yes. How soft it is. It must be cashmere or something.

David: Eh, I think it's a mixture of wool and silk, actually. I'm going to give it to my mother-in-law. They're her sort of colours.

Anne: And what about this tool-kit? I suppose that's for Tom and that old banger he's got?

David: Well, no. I bought that for my mother, actually. She's always saying she wants one for the car and never gets round to buying one. I'm not surprised, the price it cost.

Anne: How much was it? I could do with one myself.

David: It was fifteen pounds I think. Look there's the label – fifteen pounds thirty.

Anne: Gosh.

David: And then I got this pair of pyjamas. Aren't they wonderful? They're silk, just like the ones in that TV ad. I got them for my brother. Do you think he'll like them?

Anne: Um, well. I bet they cost a fortune.

David: Um, yes. Forty pounds.

Anne: Well, he'd better like them, hadn't he? I think your budget isn't in the same bracket as mine.